DROP THE ROPE

DROP THE ROPE

You're Not Overreacting.

You're Over-Explaining.

Dr. Renea Skelton

First edition, 2026

Printed in the United States of America

Hardcover ISBN: 978-1-7349096-7-8

Paperback ISBN: 978-1-7349096-8-5

Published by Harmony Harbor Publications

www.reneaskelton.com

For John, who let me practice dropping the rope even when I picked it back up.

For Kelcie, Chloe, and Wesley, who remind me daily that love does not need defending.

And for Carolyn, who understood this long before I could name it.

Table of Contents

FOREWORD

I was deeply honored to write the foreword to Drop the Rope.

As someone who spends much of my time inspiring others to define their own path to financial freedom, I can honestly say this book is pure gold.

Not only was I privileged to be among the first to read it, but my notebook, now full of notes and reflections, is evidence of how much this book has already blessed me. I have grown because of it. After the very first chapter, I immediately began practicing the art of "dropping the rope" and assessing how this new skill was reshaping my responses, my peace, and my perspective.

Before reading this book, I believed I knew how to "command" every situation. As a retired Air Force officer, I assumed I already had the tools to navigate conflict and difficult conversations. Yet as I read, I realized that leadership alone does not always equip us for the emotional and relational challenges we face.

As a devoted spouse and as a mother of two teenage daughters, I discovered I also had room to grow. With each chapter, I found myself peeling back layers like an onion and confronting truths that were sometimes uncomfortable, sometimes tender, and ultimately healing.

I laughed. I cried. I paused. I reflected. There were moments I had to pick the book up just to avoid sending a text I know I should not send.

This book is for you if you have ever spoken too quickly, defended too strongly, or engaged in a battle, even in your mind, that cost you your peace. It gives you permission to pause, breathe, and choose differently.

Do not put this book down until you have fully embraced the freedom that comes with dropping the rope.

— Janelle Just Quinn

Co-Author of *Soul Talk Volume 4,* #1 Amazon Best Seller

Founder, 3FIVE Wealth™

INTRODUCTION

Why We Keep Pulling

Let me tell you what finally broke me.

It wasn't a screaming fight. It wasn't betrayal. It wasn't some dramatic, cinematic moment where everything shattered and I swore to become a calmer, more enlightened person.

It was a Tuesday.

A completely average, unremarkable Tuesday where someone said something small - not cruel, not outrageous, just small - and I felt it. That shift. That tightening. That immediate internal lean forward like my entire body was preparing to defend something that technically wasn't under attack.

Before I knew it, I was explaining.

Explaining my reasoning. Explaining my tone. Explaining why I did what I did. Explaining what I meant. Explaining what I didn't mean. Explaining so thoroughly that by the end of it, no one was arguing with me anymore... but I still felt like I'd lost something.

Energy. Peace. Dignity. Something.

The conversation ended. I walked away. And then I kept having it in my head for the next three hours while unloading the dishwasher.

That's when it hit me.

Why am I still holding this?

Why am I acting like every comment is a rope being handed to me - and my only job is to grab it and start pulling?

That's what it feels like, doesn't it?

Someone says something that lands sideways. You feel the pull. You grab. Now you're in it. Tug-of-war over meaning, over tone, over who's right, over what was implied, over whether you're being misunderstood, disrespected, underestimated, mischaracterized, dismissed.

It rarely starts big. It starts tiny.

It costs more than we realize.

I Was Really Good at Pulling

Here's the part that's mildly embarrassing.

I teach communication for a living.

I've stood in front of rooms full of leaders. I've trained professionals on emotional intelligence. I've built workshops around clarity, boundaries, and self-awareness. I spent over two decades in the military, where composure and control aren't optional traits.

And yet.

I could still find myself defending why I ordered something a certain way at a drive-thru, narrating my choices like the barista was about to file a formal complaint about my character.

"I'm not being difficult, it's just -"

Hmph. No one asked.

I could still rewrite texts three times to make sure they sounded firm but not cold, clear but not aggressive, confident but not arrogant, warm but not overly apologetic. I'd hit send and immediately feel the urge to send another one clarifying the first one.

I could still walk away from a simple conversation and replay it like it had been recorded for review.

For someone who understood communication conceptually, I was exhausting myself relationally.

I know I'm not alone.

What It Was Costing Me

This isn't just about arguments. It's about the constant low-grade tension of being on guard.

It's about walking into rooms already braced.

It's about rehearsing conversations that haven't happened yet.

It's about explaining yourself before anyone questions you.

It's about over-clarifying because somewhere along the way you learned that being misunderstood was dangerous.

It's about lying in bed at night thinking of better ways you could have said something that didn't need saying in the first place.

That mental tug-of-war doesn't just waste time. It drains your nervous system. It keeps you slightly activated, slightly defensive, and slightly vigilant.

Over time, slightly tired.

I didn't need better comebacks. I needed to stop pulling.

Where "Drop the Rope" Came From

The phrase came out of my mouth before I fully understood it.

I was in the middle of coaching someone who was explaining - passionately, intelligently, thoroughly - why they were right in a situation that had already ended. They were building a case no one was arguing against anymore.

I heard myself say, "You don't have to keep pulling the rope."

We both paused because that's exactly what it was.

No one was forcing them to argue. No one was demanding the defense. The rope was just... there. Familiar. Automatic.

They had picked it up.

I had picked it up.

We *all* pick it up.

The moment you see it that way, something shifts. Because if it's a rope, you don't have to cut it. You don't have to burn it. You don't have to prove you can win.

You *can* put it down.

That's it.

What This Book Is - And What It Isn't

This is not a book about becoming silent.

It's not about tolerating disrespect. It's not about being passive. It's not about pretending you don't care.

You care. That's why you pull.

This is about learning the difference between responding and reacting. Between clarity and control. Between boundaries and defensiveness.

It's about noticing the moment your body leans forward and deciding whether that moment actually deserves your energy.

Some conversations matter. Some absolutely require you to speak.

But most of the time, what we're fighting isn't the other person. It's the feeling of being misread.

That feeling doesn't require combat. It requires awareness.

I Still Grab It Sometimes

Let's be clear. I am not rope-free 24/7.

There are days when I am tired, overstimulated, under-caffeinated, or surprised by someone who knows exactly which sentence will activate me.

There are moments when I hear myself mid-explanation and think, Oh no. We're doing this again.

There are texts I almost send. There are comments I draft and delete. There are times when I feel the pull and grab it anyway because being human sometimes outruns being intentional.

The difference now is not perfection. It's recovery.

It's catching it faster. It's dropping it sooner.

It's not spending three days replaying what could have been one imperfect moment.

That shift changed my life more than any communication technique ever did.

Why You're Here

If you picked up this book, you're probably tired.

Tired of defending yourself in conversations that shouldn't feel like debates.

Tired of replaying moments that technically ended.

Tired of explaining things no one asked you to explain.

Tired of caring this much about how something landed.

You're not dramatic and you're not too sensitive. You're holding something you don't need to carry.

The rope will still show up. In relationships. In work. In family. In text threads. In comment sections. In tiny comments that shouldn't matter but somehow do.

The goal isn't to eliminate the rope. The goal is to recognize that you don't have to grab it just because it's there.

This book will walk you through what that looks like - in your body, in your words, in your relationships, in the quiet moments after the conversation ends.

Not perfectly and not all at once.

But enough.

Enough to feel lighter.

Enough to stop living like you're constantly on the defensive.

Enough to reclaim the energy you've been spending on battles that didn't need to happen.

You don't need a better comeback.

You need to stop pulling.

Let's begin.

PART I

SEEING THE GAME

1

SPOTTING THE ROPE

That Tiny Moment Before You Start Explaining

I did not plan to write a book about tug-of-war dynamics. I did not wake up one morning with a grand theory about ego and nervous systems. I was standing in my kitchen, annoyed at a frying pan, and somehow that was enough.

It was a weeknight. I was tired in that very specific way where nothing is technically wrong, but everything feels slightly heavier than it should. I had agreed to cook dinner even though I did not particularly want to cook dinner, which already put me in a delicate emotional state. The only clean pan in the cabinet was not the right size for what I was making, but instead of washing another one like a reasonable person, I decided to *make* it work. Not because it was the best choice but because it was the easiest one.

The food was crowded. The oil was popping. Not aggressively. Just enough to feel personal. I stood there nudging the food around in the pan that was clearly overcrowded, trying to convince myself that this was fine. It was fine. Nothing was burning. Nothing was catastrophic. This was just what dinner looked like when you were determined to push through instead of recalibrating.

If you have ever been in that mood where you are already doing something you do not want to be doing and you are telling yourself it is fine, you know how thin that emotional margin is. You are not calm. You are contained.

Then my husband walked into the kitchen, glanced at the stove, and said in the most neutral, reasonable voice imaginable, "Why are you using a small pan?"

That was it.

No tone. No criticism. No follow-up comment from him.

And yet my body reacted like he had just said, "Do you have any idea what you're doing?"

Before I even turned around, my chest tightened. My jaw set. My shoulders lifted slightly as if preparing for impact. My brain, which had been sluggish all day, suddenly came online like it had been waiting for something to defend.

Because it was *not* about the pan.

It was about the fact that I was already irritated. It was about the fact that I was trying to make something work without admitting it wasn't working. It was about the fact that I did not want help but also did not want his commentary. It was about the fact that I felt stretched thin and suddenly very visible.

And what did I do with all of that nuanced internal complexity?

I started explaining the pan.

I explained that the larger one was dirty. I explained that I was already halfway through. I explained that it was fine and that I had it handled. I explained it with the tone of someone presenting evidence in a courtroom, as if the cookware choice might otherwise permanently damage my credibility.

Halfway through, I was aware that I was overexplaining. There was a tiny voice inside me that knew this was excessive. *We are not negotiating a merger. We are cooking chicken.* But once I had started, it felt impossible to stop. The explanation had momentum. My nervous system had decided this was important.

My husband, meanwhile, had already moved on. He was not escalating and he was not offended. He had asked a practical question and was now living his life.

I was the only one still in the arena. And that is when it hit me later that night.

I was not protecting dinner. I was protecting my image.

I did not want to be seen as careless or inefficient. Or like someone who could not manage something as basic as cookware. Which is absurd when you say it out loud, but in the moment it felt deeply reasonable. Necessary, even. I was not trying to win an argument. I was trying to make sure no one left the room thinking I was incompetent with sautéed vegetables.

If that sounds dramatic, welcome to the rope.

The rope does not show up in epic battles. It shows up in tiny moments where your body decides something is at stake. It is the invisible tension between what was said and what you think it means. It is the split second where "Why are you using a small pan?" becomes "You don't know what you're doing," and your system reacts before your logic can catch up.

That translation happens fast. Faster than fairness. Faster than context.

Later that evening, when the house was quiet, I replayed it. Not obsessively. Just enough to notice the shift. There had been a clear moment between his question and my response where something tightened inside me. That was the rope appearing.

I had grabbed it automatically.

And if I was honest, this was not new.

I had done this in grocery store checkout lines when someone glanced at my cart, and I felt the need to mentally justify frozen pizza like I was submitting a dietary report.

I had done this when I was five minutes late and arrived with a preloaded explanation no one asked for.

I had done this in meetings when a casual suggestion felt like a critique of my entire competence.

I had even done this with my dog, explaining why his dinner was late as if he was silently evaluating my performance.

He was not. He wanted food.

But the pattern was the same.

A neutral moment.

A body reaction.

An internal story.

An explanation.

Every time, it felt responsible. Mature. Communicative. I was *just* making sure things were clear. I was *just* preventing misunderstanding. I was *just* advocating for myself.

What I was actually doing was *pulling*.

The rope convinces you that clarification equals control. It tells you that if you explain clearly enough, the moment will settle and everyone will understand you exactly as you intend to be understood. It whispers that silence would be irresponsible and that if you do not intervene, the wrong version of you will linger in the room.

And here is the part no one likes admitting: most of the time, no one was forming a case against you in the first place.

They were thinking about themselves. While you were mentally drafting a defense over cookware. When I finally saw it clearly, I did not feel shame. I felt tired.

I was tired of the constant internal tightening and of the subtle performance. I was also tired of managing perception in rooms where nothing dangerous was actually happening.

The rope had been there for years. I just had not named it.

That night in the kitchen, oil popping and ego flaring, I realized I had been playing tug-of-war in moments that did not require a game.

The pan was too small. But the reaction was much bigger. And that was the first time I saw the rope in my hands.

2

THE EGO GRIP

Why Being "Right" Feels Safer Than Being Calm

If the frying pan was the moment I noticed the rope, what came next was less about cookware and more about what was actually tightening inside me.

Because here's the uncomfortable truth: the rope doesn't grip your hands first. It grips your *identity*.

You can tell yourself the reaction was about tone or timing or delivery, but if you slow it down enough, what's really happening is that something about the comment brushes against who you believe yourself to be. Not the public version... the internal résumé. The part of you that keeps a quiet record of your effort, your competence, your thoughtfulness, your sacrifice.

When my husband asked about the pan, my reaction wasn't about stainless steel. It was about the possibility that I was being seen as careless. That I might look like someone who didn't think ahead. That maybe I was sloppy, inefficient, and not on top of things.

None of those words were spoken.

My body supplied them.

That's *ego.*

Before you picture someone loud and arrogant and obsessed with being right, pause. This is not ego in the peacocking sense. This is ego in the protective sense. Ego as security system. Ego as internal PR department. Ego as the slightly dramatic friend who believes every raised eyebrow is a threat to your reputation.

Ego doesn't wake up thinking, "How can I dominate today?" It wakes up thinking, "Let's make sure no one misreads us."

Somewhere along the way, being misread cost you something. Maybe it was as small as being teased. Maybe it was being dismissed. Maybe it was not being taken seriously. Maybe it was being told you were too sensitive when you were actually paying attention.

Your nervous system remembers that.

So now when someone says, "We might need to rethink this," your body doesn't hear collaboration. It hears, "You missed something." When someone says, "That's interesting," your brain runs it through seventeen tonal filters trying to determine whether "interesting" means curious or quietly unimpressed.

You can watch yourself doing it and still not stop.

I once caught myself overexplaining an email that no one had criticized. A colleague had replied with a simple, "Can we adjust this slightly?" That was it. No accusation. No edge. It was simply a suggestion.

Within seconds, my brain was constructing a detailed narrative explaining my reasoning, the context behind the decision, the timeline constraints, and the strategic considerations that had gone into a two-sentence paragraph.

The adjustment could have been made in under a minute. Instead, I felt compelled to defend the thinking behind it, as if the suggestion meant someone believed I hadn't thought at all.

That is the ego grip. It's subtle. It's fast. It's convincing. It tells you that you're not defending yourself, you're clarifying.

You're not reacting, you're communicating. You're not protecting your image, you're protecting accuracy. And technically, you are. But the urgency underneath it tells a different story.

Ego does not like ambiguity. It does not like the idea that someone might walk away with an incomplete or inaccurate version of you. It would prefer to overexplain than risk being misunderstood. It would rather flood the room with context than sit in the discomfort of uncertainty.

And the thing about ego is that it sounds exactly like you.

It uses your voice, your logic, even your values. It doesn't announce itself with dramatic flair. It blends in so seamlessly that you mistake it for discernment.

You tell yourself you are standing up for yourself. Sometimes you are. But sometimes you are simply standing guard over an identity that feels fragile in the moment.

If you want to see ego in action, watch what happens when someone implies you didn't try hard enough.

You might not explode. You might not even look upset. But internally something shifts. Your brain starts listing evidence. *I did try. I stayed up late. I thought about this. I put effort into this.* You can feel the heat rise in your chest as if you are about to present exhibits A through Z.

What you're really defending is not the task. It's the story about who you are.

Ego is efficient. It reacts before you have fully formed the thought. It reads between lines that may not exist. It interprets pauses as judgments. It prefers certainty, even if it has to manufacture it.

Being wrong and being unsafe can feel identical in your body.

Logically, you know that feedback does not threaten your existence. You may also know that a suggestion does not erase your competence. But your nervous system doesn't operate on logic. It operates on perceived threat. So, when someone questions a decision, even gently, your body reacts first and your brain follows with justification.

That's why you can walk away from a conversation that ended fine and still feel unsettled. That's why you replay small exchanges while brushing your teeth. That's why you think of better responses in the shower three hours later.

You are not dramatic. You are protecting identity.

The ego grip tightens most around the roles that matter to you. If you pride yourself on being thoughtful, any implication that you weren't will sting. If you value competence, even a neutral suggestion can feel like a quiet indictment. If you see yourself as generous, the slightest hint that you didn't do enough can feel disproportionately heavy.

You don't react to everything. You react to what touches your self-definition. And once you see that, the pattern becomes clearer.

It's not random.

It's not personality.

It's *protection.*

The tricky part is that ego believes explanation equals control. If you can just say it clearly enough, thoroughly enough, convincingly enough, then you can lock in the right narrative. You can prevent the wrong interpretation from sticking.

Except you can't actually control how someone else understands you. You can influence it. You can clarify. You can speak. But you cannot guarantee it.

Ego hates that. It would rather overwork you than sit with the idea that someone might misunderstand you and survive.

The more I started noticing the ego grip, the more I saw how often it showed up in small moments. Not dramatic arguments or the major conflicts. Just tiny identity flares that felt like they needed immediate tending.

I realized that half the time I wasn't defending myself from attack. I was defending myself from implication. That realization was both humbling and freeing. Humbling because it meant I was not as detached as I thought I was. Freeing because once you see the ego grip, you can pause before it fully tightens.

The rope does not appear because you are weak. It appears because something in you wants to be seen accurately.

The problem is not that you care. The problem is that ego convinces you that caring requires pulling. And that is where the exhaustion begins.

3

CHOOSING NOT TO PULL

The Pause That Changes Everything

The first time you intentionally choose not to pull the rope, it does not feel like wisdom. It feels like you forgot to finish something.

There's a moment in a conversation when something lands slightly off. It's not wrong, aggressive, and not even clearly critical. It's angled enough that your nervous system leans forward and your brain quietly begins preparing a response. You can feel the shift before you can name it. Your chest tightens in that small, familiar way. Your jaw firms up just slightly. Your mind starts arranging words as if it has already decided they will be needed.

You are not trying to win anything, and you are not trying to dominate. You are trying to prevent a misunderstanding before it hardens into something that will sit wrong later. The urge to clarify feels responsible. It feels like good communication. It feels like maturity. You tell yourself that emotionally intelligent people address things in real time. Emotionally intelligent people don't let tension linger.

And yet, for reasons that surprise even you, you don't speak.

You notice the tightening instead of obeying it. You feel the words lining up behind your teeth and you let them wait. The other person continues talking. The room does not collapse. The ceiling does not cave in. No one gasps at your silence.

But inside your body, it feels unfinished.

Your brain does not appreciate this new experiment. It begins offering you reasons why you should just add a sentence. It would only take a few seconds. You could make it lighter. Clearer. Safer.

You could make sure they understood what you meant. You could avoid having to think about this later tonight while brushing your teeth. Because that's the real threat, isn't it? Not the moment itself. The replay.

Pulling relieves the pressure immediately. It gives your nervous system something to do. It makes the discomfort feel productive.

When you explain, you feel like you're securing the narrative. You're locking it in. You're preventing the wrong interpretation from floating away unchecked.

Not pulling means sitting in the possibility that someone might misunderstand you and surviving that possibility anyway.

That is deeply uncomfortable.

The first few times I practiced this, it felt like I was holding my breath underwater. I would feel the urge rise, feel my body lean forward, and then deliberately choose to stay still. Not passive. Not resentful. Just aware.

My brain would begin assembling arguments in the background. It reminded me of every time silence had backfired. It suggested that staying quiet could look like agreement. It warned me that if I didn't clarify now, I would regret it later. It sounded logical and protective. It sounded almost noble.

It took me a while to realize that my brain was not responding to the situation. It was responding to the discomfort.

There is a difference between clarity and compulsion. Clarity feels steady. Compulsion feels urgent. Compulsion wants relief now. It does not want to wait and see whether the moment resolves itself naturally. It wants control. It wants to manage perception before perception even fully forms.

When you choose not to pull, you are not choosing silence as a personality trait. You are choosing timing. You are choosing to respond from steadiness instead of from activation. You are allowing the moment to breathe before you rush in to manage it.

That breathing room is everything.

I remember sitting in a meeting where someone casually suggested adjusting a piece of a project I had spent hours refining. The suggestion was neutral. Thoughtful, even. But my body reacted as if my competence had just been placed on trial. I could feel the list of justifications lining up behind my eyes. I had reasons for every decision. I had context. I had strategic thinking that no one else in the room could possibly appreciate without a brief presentation.

In other words, I was ready.

Instead, I paused. I let the suggestion land without immediately defending my work. I listened. Not to tone. Not to implication. To content. And here is the part that makes me laugh now: the adjustment made it better.

If I had launched into defense, I would have missed that. I would have been so focused on protecting my image as "thoughtful and thorough" that I wouldn't have heard the actual value being offered.

Choosing not to pull does not make you weak. It makes you available. Available to reality instead of reaction.

This practice shows up in places that are almost comical once you start noticing them. You walk into a room five minutes late and feel the urge to narrate your commute as if someone is waiting to issue a citation. No one says a word but you begin explaining anyway.

Choosing not to pull in that moment looks like sitting down without delivering a traffic report. It feels exposed at first, as though someone might silently think you're irresponsible. Most of the time, no one is thinking that at all.

Or you send an email and receive a simple, "Can we tweak this?" The urge to respond with three paragraphs explaining your thought process rises immediately. Choosing not to pull might look like making the tweak and moving on, without attaching a thesis to your original draft.

It feels incomplete. It also feels lighter.

The more you practice staying in that small gap between urge and action, the more you realize how often you were acting from tension rather than clarity. You begin to see how much energy was being spent on micro-defenses. How many conversations you were subtly bracing for. How often you were performing competence instead of simply being competent.

Over time, the gap widens. Not because the urge disappears. It doesn't. The rope still appears and the ego still flares. The internal story still tries to form. But you recognize it sooner. You feel the tightening and think, *There it is.*

You don't have to grab it just because it showed up.

The first time you let the urge crest and fall without acting on it, you may still feel unsettled afterward. That's normal. Your system is used to relieving discomfort through explanation. When you interrupt that habit, it feels foreign.

But if you stay with it long enough, something else emerges.

Relief.

Not dramatic relief and not the kind that changes your life in a single conversation. Just the quiet realization that the moment passed without you having to manage it. That the room did not implode and that your identity remained intact without a formal defense.

You begin to understand that not every internal flare requires an external response. Some require awareness. Some require patience. Some require nothing at all.

Choosing not to pull is not about silence. It is about freedom from automatic reaction. It is about discovering that the urge to clarify is a sensation, not a command.

The more often you practice that pause, the more you experience conversations differently. You listen more fully because you are not busy rehearsing. You respond more intentionally because you are not scrambling. You walk away from interactions and leave them there instead of carrying them home like unfinished business.

The rope still exists.

You just no longer feel obligated to pick it up every time it's offered.

PART II

WHERE IT SHOWS UP

4

DROPPING THE ROPE AT HOME

When the Shoes Aren't Actually the Problem

You don't notice the shoes at first.

You walk in carrying too many things because you *always* carry too many things. Your bag, your keys, something from the car you didn't technically need to grab right now but did anyway because if you don't, no one else will. You're mid-thought about something from earlier when your foot catches on something soft and rubbery and you nearly do that awkward half-stumble that somehow feels both dramatic and deeply undignified.

You look down.

There they are.

A sneaker tipped on its side like it fainted. A boot half on the mat and half off as if it tried to comply with basic house standards but lost motivation halfway through. Slides kicked in opposite directions like they broke up and are refusing to co-parent the entryway.

You just stand there.

Nothing is burning. No one is yelling. There is no crisis. Just shoes.

And yet something in your chest tightens like this is Exhibit Q in a case you did not realize you've been quietly building.

It would take ten seconds to fix it. Maybe eight if you're efficient. You have picked up these exact shoes before. Your hands know their weight. You know which shelf they belong on without looking. You could fix this and move on, and no one would even know it ever happened.

That's the point.

No one would even know.

You glance into the living room where everyone else is seated. Relaxed. Existing. Fully unaware that the house runs on a constant, invisible noticing system and that you are the operating system.

It isn't about the shoes.

It's about the fact that no one else paused. It's about the mental list running in the background of your brain at all times. The list that tracks groceries, appointments, birthdays, school emails, the sound the dishwasher made yesterday that didn't sound normal, the fact that someone is almost out of toothpaste, the towel that's still in the dryer, the trash day that's tomorrow. You see the things before they become problems.

You are the early warning system and early warning systems are rarely thanked.

So, when you almost trip over a sneaker that could have been placed literally six inches to the left, your nervous system does something disproportionate to the situation. Not explosive and not theatrical. Just a small internal shift that says, *I see everything, and no one sees that I see everything.*

That's when the rope shows up at home.

Home is where you expect to stop performing. It's where you assume you don't have to explain yourself. It's the place where you should be known enough that you don't need to defend your effort or narrate your contribution.

Which is why the smallest thing can feel like the biggest insult. Because when it happens at home, it feels personal.

If a stranger leaves their shoes in the middle of a public walkway, you might roll your eyes and step around them. If someone you live with does it for the hundredth time, your body reacts like this is evidence in a long-standing case about who carries what around here.

You pick up the damn shoes.

Of course you do.

You slide them into place and straighten the mat. You take a breath you didn't realize you were holding. Then someone from the couch says casually, "You okay?"

Not accusatory nor cruel. Just curious. Somehow that question feels like the final insult because you're not just the one who notices. You're the one who is "overreacting."

You hear yourself say, "I'm fine," but your tone betrays you slightly. It's thinner than you meant it to be and it carries a small charge. They pick up on it.

"What's wrong?"

Now the rope is fully in your hands.

You could say, "Nothing," and swallow it. You could say, "It's just the shoes, and make it about footwear like this is a simple domestic disagreement about organization." Or you could do what most of us do, which is explain the entire invisible ecosystem of noticing that has been running in the background of your life for years.

You're not yelling. You're clarifying.

You're not attacking. You're explaining.

You start listing but not in a dramatic way - in a measured, reasonable way. You mention the laundry you folded earlier. The email you sent. The trash you took out. The fact that you are the one who keeps track of everything that doesn't get tracked.

You're not wrong. That's what makes it dangerous. The conversation is no longer about shoes. It's about contribution, about effort, and about who sees what and who doesn't. It's about fairness disguised as footwear.

At home, the rope is rarely about the moment in front of you. It's about the accumulation of moments behind you.

Your partner hears criticism. You hear invisibility.

They defend their effort. You defend yours.

You both start reaching for receipts from the past like you're in a courtroom no one agreed to attend.

The rope tightens.

The people who live with you have seen you at your most unfiltered. They've seen you tired, irritated, brilliant, unreasonable, generous, quiet, loud. They know which comments land and which one's sting. They don't always mean to use that knowledge, but sometimes they do without realizing it.

When someone at home says, "You don't have to do everything," it doesn't feel like support. It feels like a suggestion that you are choosing this, that you are voluntarily running a mental marathon no one asked you to run.

So, you pull.

You explain that if you don't do it, it doesn't get done. You clarify that you're not asking for applause, you're asking for awareness. You list examples because you want accuracy. You want to make sure the record reflects reality.

But here's what makes the rope at home different from everywhere else: the stakes feel higher because the closeness is deeper.

When a coworker misreads you, it's annoying. When someone you love misreads you, it feels like erosion. It feels like, *You should know me by now.*

Which is why dropping the rope at home feels almost unnatural at first. It feels like not defending yourself is agreeing with something untrue. It feels like silence equals surrender. But most of the time, the other person is not building a case against you. They're not silently tallying your flaws and they're not conducting a private performance review of your character.

They're simply existing.

The **mental load** rope lives here too.

You are the one who knows when the dog is due for shots. You remember the neighbor's name. You know which kid prefers which cup. You anticipate the chaos before it unfolds and quietly intercept it.

When someone asks, "What needs to be done?" it doesn't feel like teamwork. It feels like proof that you're the only one running the map.

You want to explain the map. Show them the map. Hand them the map. You want them to understand the sheer volume of invisible coordination happening at all times. And yet explaining it doesn't lighten it. It just adds another task.

Dropping the rope at home sometimes looks like letting the shoes stay there. Not forever and not dramatically – only long enough for someone else to notice them. Long enough for the absence of your silent cleanup to create awareness.

That feels reckless the first time you do it.

You will stand in the hallway, staring at those shoes like they are a social experiment. You will fight the urge to fix it. You will hear a voice in your head saying, *This is childish. Just pick them up.*

And then you won't.

Something strange will happen. Either someone else will pick them up, or they will step over them and eventually trip and suddenly see what you've been seeing all along.

Visibility doesn't come from explanation. It comes from space.

Dropping the rope at home doesn't mean you stop caring. It means you stop managing how you are perceived in every single moment.

It means when someone asks, "You okay?" you can say, "I'm tired," and leave it there without attaching a footnote and a supporting document.

It means when you're misunderstood, you don't always sprint to correct the record.

It means you trust that one uncorrected moment won't define your entire contribution to the household.

Home is where the rope shows up most often because home is where you are most exposed. It's where dropping the rope matters most because the people who live with you don't need the defended version of you - they need the honest one.

Sometimes honest looks like saying less.

Sometimes it looks like picking up the shoes without building a case.

Sometimes it looks like not picking them up at all.

Sometimes it looks like standing in the hallway, staring at a sneaker on its side, realizing that you are about to start a war over rubber and laces, and deciding instead that maybe - just maybe - this doesn't need to be the hill you die on.

The shoes were never the enemy.

The rope was.

5

DROPPING THE ROPE AT WORK

Performance, Perception, and the Panic to Prove Yourself

Work is where competence and identity quietly start sharing a bank account.

At home, you can have a bad day and still be loved. You can burn dinner, forget something, overreact about shoes, and most likely, someone will still sit next to you on the couch later. At work, love is not part of the agreement. Value is. Output is. Performance reviews are.

Somewhere between your first paycheck and your first promotion, you begin to absorb a belief that feels logical but isn't entirely true: if you are good at your job, then you are good. Full stop.

So, when someone questions your work, your body does not register, "Interesting perspective." It registers something much bigger and much louder.

It registers, "You don't belong here."

The rope appears fast in professional spaces because work taught you that visibility equals safety and silence can equal invisibility. You learned that being overlooked is risky. You learned that the quiet one sometimes gets passed over. You learned that the person who cannot explain themselves fluently may be labeled as unprepared.

None of that makes you insecure. It makes you trained.

The rope at work rarely looks dramatic. It does not slam doors or raise voices. It wears neutral colors and schedules follow-ups. It says, "Just to clarify," in a tone that sounds calm but is vibrating internally. It looks like professionalism. It sounds like thoroughness. It feels responsible.

Underneath, it is the same pull.

You are not simply doing your job. You are performing your capability.

Every email is subtle evidence. Every meeting is a quiet evaluation. Every follow-up question feels like a micro-audit of whether you actually know what you're doing or whether you have somehow been faking adulthood convincingly for years.

You begin over-preparing for conversations that may never happen. You anticipate objections before anyone has objected. You write context into emails no one requested because you want to make sure there is no possible interpretation where you look careless. You call this being proactive. Sometimes it is. Sometimes it is your nervous system building a defense before anyone has attacked.

The rope convinces you that more explanation equals more credibility. If you can just give enough reasoning, enough background, enough logic, then no one will doubt you. If you can remove every gap, you can remove every risk.

What actually happens is subtler and more ironic.

The more you explain, the less steady you sound. The more you justify, the more defensive you appear. The longer your email, the more likely it is that someone will read the first three lines and reply with, "Thanks," having missed the entire masterpiece you constructed to prove you are competent.

Competence does not require constant demonstration. Insecurity does.

One of the most common places the rope tightens at work is around feedback.

Someone says, "We might need to rethink this approach," and your body responds like you've just been placed on trial in front of a jury that controls your mortgage. Your mind races. You replay your preparation. You begin internally listing every factor you considered. You want to walk them through your entire thought process, so they know you are not careless, not sloppy, not guessing.

What you are really saying underneath the explanation is, "Please don't reduce me to this one moment."

But most feedback is not a verdict. It is collaboration and perspective. It is someone doing their job, not dismantling your identity.

The problem is that your nervous system does not separate critique of the work from critique of you. At work, your output and your worth sit too close together. When someone critiques the output, your body assumes your worth is also on the table.

If you cannot separate those two things, every conversation becomes defensive and every meeting becomes performative.

Every email becomes evidence you are compiling in case someone someday questions whether you belong.

That is exhausting.

There is also the **comparison** rope, which thrives in conference rooms and open floor plans.

You notice the person who speaks confidently without notes. The one who answers questions without pausing. The one who seems unfazed when challenged. You assume they feel solid inside. You assume they do not lie awake thinking about that one comment they made in the meeting at 2:17 p.m. that might have sounded slightly off.

You compensate.

You rehearse answers in your head. You monitor your tone and try to sound confident but not arrogant, collaborative but not weak, decisive but not rigid. You adjust constantly, like you are tuning yourself in real time to match an invisible standard.

The rope does not disappear because you are prepared. It appears because you are attached to certainty as protection. You believe that if you are airtight enough, you cannot be doubted.

Here is something freeing and slightly uncomfortable: some people at work are simply comfortable being wrong and they are comfortable being questioned. They do not treat every disagreement as a vote on their competence.

That is not arrogance. That is detachment.

Dropping the rope at work often means allowing yourself to be human in a space that rewards the appearance of being flawless. You do not have to be the person who never stumbles.

You only need to be the person who does not spiral when you do.

Let's talk about email, because email is where the rope quietly does cardio.

You send a clear message. It makes sense. You reread it twice. You feel good about it.

Then someone replies with, "Can you clarify this part?" That is all they say. Your brain supplies the rest.

They didn't understand. I was unclear. This looks sloppy. Now I have to prove that I thought this through.

Instead of answering the question directly, you write a defense and add background. You reference prior conversations and justify decisions that were not challenged. You build a narrative that explains your competence from childhood to present day.

By the time you hit send, you feel like you have defended a thesis no one assigned.

They read the first paragraph and respond with, "Got it, thanks."

That is the rope.

The question was not an accusation. Your nervous system just treated it like one.

Dropping the rope in email is almost painfully simple. It looks like answering the question that was asked. It looks like trusting that clarity is enough. It looks like resisting the urge to attach a protective essay to every response.

It feels risky because you are not managing perception in every exchange. You are trusting your competence to stand without you constantly holding it up.

Meetings hand you the rope in public.

Someone pushes back on your idea. Not aggressively nor dramatically. Just enough to create friction. Your body reacts instantly. The urge to jump in and reinforce your thinking becomes overwhelming. You begin adding detail. You preempt objections that have not been raised. You escalate the energy of the moment because it feels like if you do not defend this immediately, the room will quietly downgrade you.

The room does not downgrade you because of the pushback. The room shifts because of the urgency. There is steadiness in letting your idea stand without gripping it.

When someone questions it, you can say, "That's a fair point. Let me think about that." When someone disagrees, you can say, "I see it differently, but I'm open to exploring options." You can clarify once without escalating into a defense spiral.

You do not have to win the room, but you have to be clear. Winning requires everyone to agree immediately. Clarity requires you to state your perspective and tolerate that not everyone will adopt it.

There is also the rope of **agreeability**, which is polite and costly.

You do not want to be labeled difficult. You do not want to be seen as the person who complicates things. So, you nod when you disagree. You soften when you want to be firm. You say, "That works," when it actually does not.

Later, you replay the conversation and draft the response you wish you had given. You feel resentment building quietly because you did not speak.

That is still tug-of-war. You are simply pulling internally.

Dropping the rope here looks like one clear sentence delivered without apology and without hostility.

"I have concerns about this approach."

"That timeline does not work for me."

"I need more clarity before I can move forward."

It is not dramatic. It is not loud. It is not over-explained. It is simply honest.

Sometimes the stakes at work are real. Your performance does matter. Your reputation does affect opportunities. Being misunderstood can have consequences.

Dropping the rope does not mean you stop caring. It means you stop confusing reaction with protection. Reacting quickly does not make you safer. Over-explaining does not build trust. Defending yourself before you are accused does not prevent judgment.

It often invites it.

Responding from steadiness instead of urgency changes how you are perceived more than any carefully constructed defense ever will. When you trust your body of work, when you trust your track record, when you trust that one tense exchange does not define your career, something shifts inside you.

You stop auditioning for your own job.

When you stop auditioning, you sound different. You fill less silence. You stop reacting to every raised eyebrow. You write emails that are concise because they are enough. You let feedback land without immediately turning it into a referendum on your worth.

Credibility at work is not built through constant explanation. It is built through solid work and through not making every interaction feel like you are defending your existence.

The rope will still show up. In Slack messages that feel pointed. In meetings where you feel exposed. In feedback that lands slightly sideways.

You just will not grab it every time. And when you do not grab it, the room feels steadier.

So do you.

6

DROPPING THE ROPE
IN FRIENDSHIPS

Over-Explaining So They Won't Leave

Friendships are where the rope is made of guilt, and guilt is sneaky because it wears soft clothes and uses heart emojis.

It does not show up screaming. It shows up as a text you meant to answer, "when you had a minute," which turns out to be three weeks later while you are standing in the grocery store staring at yogurt like it personally betrayed you. You see their name and your stomach does that small, annoying drop that feels disproportionate to the situation, and now you are judging yourself for feeling dread about someone you genuinely love.

That is the rope. It is not loud. It is internal narration.

You tell yourself a story before they even say a word. The story says you are slipping. That you used to be better at this. That good friends do not disappear for stretches of time and then resurface with, "Sorry, life has been insane," as if that sentence fixes anything. The story says you are becoming one of those people who lets friendships fade, and that is not who you thought you were.

Meanwhile, they may just be folding laundry and assuming you are busy. But you do not know that, because you are busy prosecuting yourself.

Friendships are the only place where you will invent a scoreboard no one asked for and then lose sleep over your performance on it. You start tracking who reached out last. Who initiated plans. Who remembered the thing about the dentist appointment. Who showed up. Who canceled. You do this quietly, almost subconsciously, like your brain installed an app called *Am I Still a Good Friend* and forgot to ask you if you wanted it running in the background at all times.

The rope tightens when you realize you are the one who forgot something. Or you are the one who bailed. Or you are the one who went quiet for a stretch because life felt heavy and you did not have the emotional bandwidth to be witty, supportive, responsive, and insightful all at once.

So, you pull.

You write paragraphs explaining your absence. You list everything on your plate to prove your distance was logistical, not emotional. You reassure them you still care deeply, passionately, wholeheartedly, in case they were secretly holding a meeting about your character.

By the time you hit send, you feel drained instead of connected.

You just defended yourself in a trial that never existed.

Friendship guilt is exhausting because it convinces you that availability equals love. That consistency equals loyalty. That if you cannot show up the way you used to, something must be wrong with you. It does not leave room for seasons, capacity, exhaustion, growth, or the simple fact that you are not twenty-two anymore with three hours to dissect a text message and a group chat that functions like a second family.

There is also the moment when a friendship stops feeling easy and starts feeling like work and admitting that out loud feels like heresy.

You love them. You truly do. But now when you see their name pop up, you do not feel immediate warmth. You feel calculation. *Do I have the energy for this right now? Can I be fully present? Am I going to have to give an update that requires vulnerability I do not have access to at the moment?*

That is not cruelty. That is capacity.

The rope appears when you decide that feeling tired equals being a bad friend. So, you override yourself. You say yes when you mean maybe and maybe when you mean no. You engage when you are depleted because loyalty is supposed to look consistent, and consistent looks like effort, and effort looks like proof that you are still the same person you were when this friendship formed.

Here is the part no one likes to admit: some friendships were built on shared proximity, not shared direction. College. A job. A neighborhood. A season of life where your chaos matched their chaos so perfectly that connection felt automatic. When the season changes, the rhythm changes. The inside jokes do not land the same because you are not living inside the same daily reality. The frequency softens. The intensity shifts.

That does not mean the friendship failed. It means time moved.

Guilt will try to convince you that real friendships survive everything unchanged, as if growth is optional and seasons are irrelevant. So, you try to resurrect a version of connection that existed in a different context. You schedule dinners you do not want. You force depth that does not feel natural anymore. You keep tugging because letting it evolve feels like letting it die.

Dropping the rope in friendships sometimes means allowing evolution without drama. It means recognizing that not every friendship is meant to stay at peak intensity forever. Some are lifelong. Some are seasonal. Some are intermittent. All of them can be meaningful without all of them being constant.

Then there is the **opposite** rope, the one that shows up when something actually bothers you.

They make a comment that lands sideways. They cancel again. They minimize something important to you. It feels small, so you swallow it. You tell yourself you are being mature. That it is not worth making a thing out of. That you do not want drama.

Meanwhile, you are building a quiet museum of grievances.

You replay moments. You stack small irritations in your memory like you are preparing a slideshow for a presentation no one asked to attend. You are not pulling out loud, but you are definitely pulling inside. You are arguing with them in the shower. You are drafting speeches in your car. You are becoming slightly colder and pretending you are fine.

That is still the rope.

Dropping it does not always mean silence. Sometimes it means speaking earlier, when the irritation is still small enough to be honest instead of explosive. It means saying, "That actually bothered me," in a tone that is steady instead of sarcastic. It means trusting that the friendship can handle clarity without you cushioning it until it disappears.

The hardest rope in friendships is the one where you change and they do not know what to do with it.

You set a boundary you never set before. You stop being the friend who is always available. You stop absorbing everyone else's emotions like you are a human emotional sponge with no off switch. You stop laughing at jokes that are not funny. You stop saying yes automatically.

They notice. They might say you have changed. They might say they miss the old you. They might say you are distant, busy, different. Your instinct will be to defend yourself and explain your evolution in PowerPoint format, complete with bullet points and a timeline of growth.

You want them to understand that this is not rejection. It is expansion.

Dropping the rope here means letting them feel confused without rushing to fix it. It means trusting that real friendship makes room for growth. If the only version of you that fits inside the friendship is the overextending one, that is information.

When you stop pulling in friendships, something strange happens. The ones that were glued together by guilt begin to loosen. The ones built on mutual respect breathe easier. You stop performing friendship and start experiencing it.

You reach out because you want to, not because you are keeping score. You say no when you need to without writing a thesis about your reasons. You let conversations end naturally without forcing intensity just to prove depth.

The friendships that remain feel lighter, not because they matter less, but because they require less performance.

You are not auditioning for the role of "good friend" anymore.

You are being the friend you actually have the capacity to be.

Friendships that are real do not collapse when you drop the rope. They adjust, stretch, and meet you where you are. The ones that depended on your guilt to stay intact will strain when you stop pulling.

That is not cruelty. That is clarity.

Friendship is not supposed to feel like community service hours you are trying to complete for moral credit. It is supposed to feel mutual, breathable, honest. When guilt is the glue, resentment eventually replaces it. When honesty is the glue, connection deepens.

Dropping the rope in friendships does not mean you love people less. It means you stop sacrificing your peace to prove that you love them enough.

If that sentence makes you slightly uncomfortable, that might be the rope loosening.

Good.

7

DROPPING THE ROPE
WITH FAMILY

Old Roles, Fast Triggers, and That One Comment

Family is where the rope was handed to you before you even knew what hands were for.

You did not audition for your role. You did not negotiate your character arc. You did not sit in a conference room at age six and agree to be "the responsible one," "the sensitive one," "the dramatic one," or "the one who just needs to relax." Yet somehow, by the time you were old enough to spell your own name correctly, the part was cast and everyone memorized their lines around you.

That is what makes family rope different from every other rope.

At work, you can resign. With friends, you can drift. In romantic relationships, you chose the person at some point, which at least gives you the illusion of agency. Family, however, is the one dynamic where history is layered so thick you cannot always tell whether you are reacting to this moment or to the one from 1998 that looked suspiciously similar.

That is why it feels heavier. It is not just rope. It is rope braided with memory.

Once you are cast in a role inside a family, the system depends on you staying there. If you are the responsible one, people assume you will handle it. If you are the emotional one, people assume you will react. If you are the quiet one, they assume you will absorb. The whole structure leans on predictability, and predictability is just another word for "please do not change because we have organized ourselves around you."

The minute you do change, it feels like betrayal.

If you are the one who always says yes and you finally say no, there will be visible confusion, as if you just switched languages mid-sentence. If you are the one who keeps the peace and you suddenly refuse to mediate the annual argument about who forgot to bring the rolls in 2007, you will be accused of "starting something" simply by declining to end it.

You are not starting something. You are stepping out of a script. To the family system, those feel identical.

The rope shows up fast in those moments. Someone will say, "You're not usually like this," which sounds observational but lands corrective. Or "What's gotten into you?" as if growth is a virus. Or the classic, "You've changed," delivered in a tone that suggests this is not a compliment.

You will feel the immediate urge to explain yourself like you are presenting quarterly results. You will want to say that you are not broken, not rebelling, not having a phase. You will want to clarify that therapy did not ruin you, that boundaries are not hostility, and that choosing not to attend every gathering does not mean you secretly hate everyone.

You will want to issue a press release.

Dropping the rope with family means resisting the urge to hold a press conference about your evolution. Sometimes growth is allowed to stand there quietly and let people adjust.

Family rope is especially powerful because it drags history into the room without asking permission. A simple comment about your job can carry twenty years of undertones. A question about your parenting can feel like every subtle criticism you absorbed growing up compressed into one sentence. When your sibling interrupts you, your body does not only hear today's interruption. It hears the pattern.

That is why your reaction sometimes feels disproportionate to the moment.

It is not disproportionate. It is cumulative.

The trap is that you start arguing with the entire archive instead of the current sentence. You defend yourself against the past while standing in the present, and by the time you are finished explaining why you are not irresponsible, selfish, dramatic, or overly sensitive, everyone else thinks the conversation was about whether you are bringing a side dish.

Dropping the rope in family dynamics often means responding to what was actually said, not to what it represents.

Sometimes the comment is just a comment. Sometimes it is not. The skill is learning to tell the difference without dragging every past injury into the room like exhibits A through Z.

Then there is the rope wrapped in **concern**.

Family concern is powerful because it is framed as love. "I'm just worried about you." "I only want what's best." "I'm saying this because I care." Those sentences come wrapped in warmth and end with subtle pressure.

If you resist, you feel ungrateful. If you set a boundary, you feel cold. If you say, "I didn't ask for advice," you feel like the villain in a Hallmark movie.

So, you pull.

You over-explain your decisions and justify your lifestyle. You defend your timing, your partner, your job, your parenting, your weight, your health choices, your existence. You try to earn trust by presenting evidence that you are, in fact, a functioning adult.

What you are really saying is, "Please stop worrying so loudly that it sounds like judgment."

Here is the part that stings: you cannot regulate someone else's anxiety by explaining yourself better.

You can write the most airtight argument in the history of arguments, complete with footnotes and a bibliography, and someone who is committed to being worried will simply find a new angle.

Dropping the rope sometimes means allowing someone to stay worried.

Allowing someone to disapprove.

Allowing someone to think you are making a mistake.

That does not mean you are careless. It means you are not taking responsibility for emotions that are not yours.

There is also the guilt rope of **distance**.

No one prepares you for how complicated it feels to realize that a little space is healthier than constant proximity. Distance does not always mean dramatic cutoffs or blocked numbers. Sometimes it simply means fewer phone calls, shorter visits, or declining the invitation that you used to accept automatically.

The guilt that follows can be loud enough to drown out your own clarity. Family is supposed to be close. Family is supposed to show up. Family is supposed to stick together. You internalized those phrases so deeply that choosing space can feel like moral failure.

But here is the uncomfortable truth: closeness is not automatically healthy just because it is familial.

If every interaction leaves you tense, braced, or depleted, it is not noble to keep volunteering as tribute.

Dropping the rope with family does not mean you love them less. It means you love yourself enough to notice what costs you too much.

Some families adjust when you change. They recalibrate. They may not love it at first, but eventually they meet you where you are. Others double down. They keep tugging, keep referencing the old version of you, keep insisting that the role you played at sixteen is your eternal identity.

When that happens, you have a choice. You can keep explaining, hoping that this time your words will unlock understanding. Or you can accept that clarity does not guarantee agreement.

There is grief in that acceptance. Real grief. The kind that sits quietly in your chest when you realize that the family you needed may not be the family you have. You grieve the conversations that will never land the way you want them to. The apologies that may never come. The validation you hoped for that remains stubbornly absent.

That grief does not mean you are ungrateful. It means you are honest.

Dropping the rope with family does not erase love. It removes the performance. You stop over-functioning to keep everyone comfortable. You stop mediating conflicts that are not yours. You stop absorbing comments that chip away at you and calling it maturity. You start saying, "I'm not available for that," without following it up with a dissertation.

You may still attend the holiday dinner. You may still answer the phone. You may still show up. The difference is internal. You are not braced for battle. You are not rehearsing rebuttals in your head before dessert. You are not treating every sideways comment like a test of your worth.

You are present without being hooked. And yes, sometimes it will still be ridiculous.

Someone will still ask why you are not married yet, even if you have been married for ten years. Someone will still comment on your plate as if they are the portion control police. Someone will still bring up a decision you made in 2003 like it is breaking news.

The difference is that you no longer feel compelled to argue history.

You can smile. You can redirect. You can say, "That works for me," without elaboration. You can let a comment float past you like background noise instead of grabbing it and wrestling it to the ground.

Family rope thrives on reaction. When you stop reacting on autopilot, the dynamic shifts, even if subtly.

You do not owe family endless tolerance, constant access, or an explanation for every boundary. You owe them basic respect and basic kindness. That is, it. Shared DNA is not a lifetime pass to your nervous system.

Dropping the rope with family is not about rebellion. It is about discernment. It is about recognizing that loyalty to them cannot come at the cost of loyalty to yourself.

The rope will still show up at holidays, in group texts, in casual comments that hit old bruises. The difference is that now you will recognize it.

And recognition is freedom.

You will pause. You will decide. And sometimes, instead of gripping tighter like you have your whole life, you will simply let it hang there.

That is not cold. That is growth. And growth, even when it makes the group chat uncomfortable, is allowed.

How You Pull (Even When You Think You're Not)

Before we talk about what to do when someone else won't let go of the rope, we need to get uncomfortably honest about something.

You don't always pull dramatically.

You don't flip tables. You don't storm out of rooms. You don't start screaming matches in the middle of Thanksgiving dinner while holding a dinner roll like a weapon.

You pull politely.

You pull intelligently.

You pull in ways that look mature.

That's what makes it so sneaky.

Pulling doesn't always look like arguing. Sometimes it looks like over-explaining. Sometimes it looks like being "clear." Sometimes it looks like being very committed to making sure everyone understands exactly what you meant, what you didn't mean, what you almost meant, and what you would have meant if they had interpreted it correctly.

You know that moment when someone slightly misunderstands you and you say, "No, no, what I meant was…" and then you proceed to give a five-minute explanation that includes context from 2007? That's pulling.

When you send the follow-up text that starts with "Just to clarify…" even though the conversation technically ended? That's pulling.

When you rewrite the email three times, so you don't sound defensive, but end up sounding like you're submitting a dissertation on your own competence? That's pulling.

When you say "It's fine" but your jaw is tight enough to crack a walnut, and you hope they notice so you don't actually have to say it? That's pulling too. Silent pulling still counts.

Sometimes pulling looks like repeating yourself with slightly different wording because maybe this version will finally land. Sometimes it looks like sarcasm because sarcasm feels safer than admitting you're hurt. Sometimes it looks like going quiet and telling yourself you're being mature, while internally you're building a legal case you plan to reference at a later date.

You might even pull internally. You walk away from a conversation and reopen it in your head while brushing your teeth. You re-argue it in the shower. You imagine what you should have said. You draft responses to comments that were never going to escalate until you escalated them in your imagination.

You tell yourself you're processing.

You're pulling.

Pulling is that urge to control how you're understood right now. It's the feeling that if you don't fix this immediately, something permanent will stick to you. It's the belief that silence equals agreement and that misunderstanding equals danger.

It's also exhausting.

Here's the wild part: half the time the other person isn't even pulling that hard. They toss out a comment. They move on. They go make coffee. They forget about it entirely while you're still constructing a twelve-point rebuttal in your head.

You grab the rope before they even tighten their grip. You do it because somewhere along the way, being misread felt unsafe. So now you manage perception like it's your second job.

You defend your tone. You justify your boundaries. You apologize for your capacity. You soften your no. You cushion your feedback. You over-contextualize your decisions, so no one thinks you're careless, selfish, dramatic, cold, incompetent, or too much.

That's not weakness. That's protection. Protection can turn into compulsion if you never question it.

If you're honest, some of your longest arguments have happened entirely in your own head. Some of your most draining moments came from conversations that weren't even that serious. Some of your biggest spikes in adrenaline came from a look, a pause, or a sentence that could have meant six different things - and you chose the most threatening one.

You don't pull because you love conflict.

You pull because you hate being misunderstood.

You pull because you hate the feeling of being mischaracterized.

You pull because you think if you can just explain it right, you can finally rest.

Explaining doesn't always bring rest.

Sometimes it just tightens the rope.

PART III

WHEN IT GETS HARD

8

DROPPING THE ROPE
WITH CLIENTS

When Money, Expectations, and Identity Collide

This chapter lives in Part III for a reason. Clients don't just trigger the rope - they raise the stakes. When money, reputation, and identity are involved, the pull feels louder. This isn't about coworkers or casual conflict. This is about when your peace and your paycheck feel intertwined." There is something about getting paid that turns otherwise regulated adults into emotional acrobats.

You can drop the rope with your partner. You can pause with your sister. You can even survive Thanksgiving without delivering a courtroom defense about your life choices. And then a client emails, "I just have a few notes," and suddenly your nervous system is sprinting like it just heard a fire alarm.

It's not the notes. It's the implied verdict.

When someone pays you, the rope gets upgraded. It's no longer cotton. It's silk and steel and wrapped in your identity.

Work is where competence and worth flirt dangerously close together. Client work is where they practically move in together.

You tell yourself you're responding professionally, and sometimes you are. But sometimes you are ten seconds away from writing a five-paragraph email that begins with "Just to clarify..." and ends with your entire résumé embedded in the footer.

Let's talk about what's actually happening.

When Feedback Feels Like a Performance Review of Your Soul

A client says, "Can we tweak this section?"

Your body hears, "You missed something obvious."

They say, "This isn't quite what I envisioned."

Your brain translates, "You are not as talented as you thought."

They ask a follow-up question.

You begin assembling a defense presentation worthy of a TED Talk.

You are not only responding to the comment. You are defending the narrative you hold about yourself as competent, capable, reliable, professional, worth the rate you charge, worth the title you hold, worth the room you sit in.

That's not about the tweak. That's about identity.

When identity is threatened, the rope shows up instantly.

You start explaining your process in detail they did not request. You outline the thinking behind every decision. You remind them of the constraints they gave you. You provide context that technically makes sense but emotionally reads like, "Please don't think I'm bad at this."

They didn't think you were bad at this. Your nervous system did.

That's the difference.

The Over-Delivery Trap

There is a very specific kind of rope that only appears when someone is paying you.

It sounds like this:

"I'll just throw that in."

"I'll go ahead and add this too."

"I know it's outside scope, but it won't take long."

"I don't want to seem difficult."

Scope creep is rarely about time management. It's about fear.

Fear that if you hold a boundary, they'll decide you're not flexible.

Fear that if you say, "That's outside our agreement," they'll decide you're not generous.

Fear that if you invoice accurately, they'll decide you're expensive.

So, you over-deliver. Not because you love excellence, although you might. Somewhere deep inside, excellence feels safer than clarity. You convince yourself you're building goodwill. What you're often building is resentment and resentment is rope you're pulling silently.

The "Quick Call" Phenomenon

Let's address the myth of the quick call.

The client says, "Can we hop on a quick call?"

You say yes.

You hydrate like you're preparing for a marathon. You review all prior correspondence. You rehearse your explanations in the mirror. You prepare mentally for objections that may or may not exist.

The call lasts nine minutes.

They ask one normal question.

You respond calmly.

You hang up and your body still feels like it just ran a 5K.

That wasn't the client.

That was your nervous system bracing for evaluation.

Living rope-free with clients means noticing when you're preparing for a firing squad and the other person is just asking about formatting.

When Authority Activates Old Patterns

Here's where it cuts deeper. Clients are rarely just clients. They are authority figures with wallets.

If you grew up needing approval from authority figures, if you learned that being the reliable one kept the peace, if you learned that being impressive meant being safe, client dynamics will activate that muscle memory fast.

You may not be reacting to this person. You may be reacting to every teacher who circled your paper in red. Every boss who questioned your competence and every parent who praised achievement more than effort.

Money adds weight to that.

You don't want to disappoint.

You don't want to look incompetent.

You don't want to be "the difficult one."

So, you pull.

You smooth.

You soften.

You over-explain.

You over-prepare.

You over-correct.

All in the name of professionalism. But professionalism is not self-erasure.

The Email You Reread Twelve Times

You send the deliverable.

They respond, "Thanks."

Just that.

Thanks.

Now you are analyzing punctuation like you work for the FBI.

Was that warm?

Was that flat?

Was that passive?

Should there have been an exclamation mark?

You draft a follow-up.

"Making sure everything looks good!"

"Happy to adjust if needed!"

"Let me know if you'd like to explore additional options!"

They didn't ask.

You're not clarifying. You're fishing for reassurance.

That's rope.

Here's the uncomfortable truth: reassurance from clients will never feel like enough if you don't trust your own work first.

The Boundary Moment

Dropping the rope with clients does not mean being rigid or cold.

It means saying things like:

"That's outside our current agreement. I'm happy to quote that separately."

"I'm not available for that timeline, but I can offer this one."

"I've already incorporated the revisions we discussed."

And then stopping.

Not softening it into a paragraph.

Not apologizing for having capacity.

Not offering a discount because you feel guilty for existing.

If your value only exists when you're endlessly accommodating, it isn't value.

It's self-sacrifice.

The Clean Invoice

There is something deeply revealing about how you send invoices.

Do you apologize?

"Sorry this is late."

"Sorry it's higher than expected."

"Sorry for the reminder."

You did the work and you delivered. You fulfilled your agreement.

An invoice is not an accusation. It is a transaction.

When you feel weird sending it, that's rope tied to worth.

The Difference Between Service and Self-Abandonment

You can be generous without being drained.

You can be professional without being defensive.

You can be responsive without being reactive.

Service becomes self-abandonment when you start managing their emotions at the expense of your own clarity.

Dropping the rope with clients means:

You don't argue to prove you're right.

You don't over-deliver to prove you're worthy.

You don't over-explain to prove you're competent.

You don't panic at neutral feedback.

You respond.

From steadiness. Not survival.

What Changes

When you stop pulling with clients, something subtle but powerful shifts.

You sound calmer.

You write shorter emails.

You hold timelines cleanly.

You stop trying to read tone like it's a secret message.

You let feedback be about the work, not your identity.

Ironically, your credibility increases.

Not because you're louder - because you're grounded.

Clients feel that difference even if they can't name it.

You become someone who collaborates instead of performs.

And the ones who only valued you when you were overextending?

They self-select out.

Which is information, not failure.

Living Rope-Free in Business

Living rope-free with clients doesn't mean you stop caring.

It means you stop confusing caring with contorting.

It means you trust your expertise enough not to defend it constantly.

It means you hold your boundaries without turning them into essays.

It means you remember that being paid does not make you small.

You are not auditioning for your own business. You are running it.

That shift alone changes everything.

Yes, sometimes you will still over-explain. Sometimes you will still panic-read an email. Sometimes you will still rehearse a call like it's the Olympics.

You're human.

But now you'll notice - noticing is where freedom begins.

Drop the rope with clients, and you'll discover something unexpected.

Your work gets better. Not because you tried harder. Because you stopped working from fear. Fear, for all its productivity, was never the thing that made you good at what you do.

You were already good.

You only don't have to prove it every time someone says, "I have a few notes."

Here's the part that humbles you just enough to keep you honest: even when you show up grounded, even when you respond clearly, even when you hold boundaries without essays or apologies, some people will still keep pulling. They will question again. They will push harder. They will try to reopen what you already closed. Not because you were unclear, but because your clarity disrupts something they were benefiting from. That's when the real test begins - not whether you can speak calmly, but whether you can stay steady when someone refuses to let the rope drop.

That's what we're walking into next.

9

WHEN THE OTHER PERSON KEEPS PULLING

How to Stay Steady When They Escalate

This is the part nobody claps for.

You notice the rope. You feel the pull. You pause instead of reacting. You don't explain yourself into dehydration. You answer the actual question instead of the imaginary accusation hiding underneath it. You stay calm. You even leave the conversation feeling slightly proud of yourself, like maybe you've evolved into one of those serene people who drinks lemon water and doesn't get baited on group texts.

And then the other person pulls harder.

Not subtly nor delicately. Not in a "let's revisit this thoughtfully" kind of way. They yank like they're trying to start a stubborn lawn mower that hasn't worked since 1998. You can practically feel the emotional recoil.

That's when the doubt begins.

Maybe I handled that wrong.

Maybe I sounded cold.

Maybe dropping the rope is just code for shutting down.

Maybe I need to circle back and clarify so they don't think I'm heartless.

You replay the interaction. You analyze your tone like it's under forensic investigation. You imagine how they're describing you to someone else. You consider sending a follow-up message that begins with, "I just want to make sure we're okay," which is almost always the gateway drug back into over-explaining.

Suddenly, you are inches away from grabbing the rope again.

Here's what you have to understand in this moment: sometimes the pull was never about misunderstanding. Sometimes it was about access. Sometimes it was about influence. Sometimes it was about control.

Control does not like being retired without notice.

What It Looks Like When They Refuse to Let Go

You answer their question directly and calmly.

They respond with another question that is technically new but spiritually identical to the first one, like the original concern put on a fake mustache and came back pretending to be someone else.

You clarify once.

They reinterpret what you said as something you very clearly did not say.

You stay neutral.

They accuse you of being distant.

You set a boundary.

They react as if you just revoked their citizenship.

The conversation keeps moving but never arrives anywhere. It circles the same themes, the same accusations, the same emotional hooks. It feels like walking on a treadmill that someone secretly set to incline ten.

That is not confusion. That is a loop.

Loops are not accidents. They are systems. They keep you engaged. They keep you explaining. They keep you activated. They keep you proving.

Some people do not want resolution. They want reassurance. They want the version of you that reacts, defends, justifies, and scrambles.

That version proves they can still shift you. That their words still land hard enough to make you move.

When you stop showing up that way, they don't experience relief. They experience loss. And loss, when it's not acknowledged, often shows up as escalation.

The Addiction to Activation

Here is something that is deeply uncomfortable to admit.

Some relationships are built around tension. The push and pull are the glue. The arguing is the intimacy. The emotional spike is the bonding ritual. If you have always been the one explaining and they have always been the one questioning, that rhythm becomes normal.

If you have always been the reactive one and they have always been the one who pokes, that becomes your dance.

It may be dysfunctional, but it is familiar. And familiar feels safe, even when it is exhausting.

When you stop pulling, you disrupt the nervous system of the relationship. You are not just changing behavior. You are removing a source of stimulation. For someone who equates intensity with connection, your calm feels like withdrawal.

So, they pull harder.

They repeat themselves. They bring up old grievances that have nothing to do with the current conversation but suddenly feel extremely relevant to them. They frame your boundary as cruelty. They call your growth "distance." They say you've changed like it's a diagnosis.

You have changed. That is the point.

But to someone who relied on your over-functioning, your steadiness feels threatening.

It is hard to manipulate someone who is no longer scrambling.

When Your Calm Becomes the Crime

Here is where this gets messy.

You stop over-explaining and suddenly you are "shutting down."

You stop reacting and suddenly you are "emotionally unavailable."

You stop accommodating and suddenly you are "selfish."

People who benefited from your anxiety will experience your clarity as aggression.

That does not mean they are villains. It means the old arrangement worked for them. And if you are not careful, you will start to believe them. You will think maybe you are being rigid. Maybe you should soften it. Maybe you need to add more context. Maybe if you explain one more time, but with better lighting and softer phrasing, they will finally understand.

So, you write the paragraph.

It starts with something responsible and kind. It ends with you defending the existence of your boundary in the first place.

Congratulations. You just picked up the rope while explaining why you weren't picking up the rope.

It's advanced tug-of-war. Very sophisticated. Olympic level.

The trap at this stage is not anger. It is the urge to be understood.

The Deep Desire to Be Understood

Let's be honest about what hurts here.

You do not want them to think you are cold. You do not want them to believe you stopped caring. You do not want to be recast as the villain in a story where you were simply trying to protect your nervous system.

So, you try to help them understand.

You explain your growth. Your boundaries. Your capacity. Your therapy breakthroughs. Your emotional evolution. You give them a guided tour of your internal landscape in the hope that empathy will follow.

It often doesn't.

They are not asking for clarity. They are asking for the old version of you.

Every time you try to convince someone that your boundary is reasonable, you are negotiating something that was never supposed to be negotiated.

You can be misunderstood and still be right.

You can be called difficult and still be healthy.

You can be accused of changing and still be exactly on track.

Their discomfort is not your emergency.

What Hooks You Back In

Even when you see the pattern clearly, something pulls at you.

Hope hooks you. You hope this conversation will be the one that shifts everything. You hope this sentence will land differently. You hope they will suddenly see you as capable and calm and not in need of correction.

Guilt hooks you. You feel bad disappointing them. Bad for not fixing the tension. Bad for letting a conversation end without wrapping it in reassurance.

Fear hooks you. You worry about what happens if you do not engage. You worry about what they will say about you. You worry about being perceived as detached.

None of those feelings are instructions.

Feelings are information, not commands.

The information here is simple: you care. You wish it could be different. You wish connection did not require this level of emotional gymnastics.

Staying in the pull will not create that version of connection. It will only exhaust you while you wait.

When You Cannot Walk Away

Sometimes you cannot just leave. The person pulling is your coworker. Your co-parent. Your sibling. Your partner. The in-law who appears at every holiday like a seasonal plot twist.

You still have to be in proximity.

This is where engaged detachment becomes a skill.

You respond to what is actually said, not what is implied. You answer direct questions without adding the justification they are fishing for. You let silence exist without rushing to rescue it. You remain polite without being emotionally hooked.

It feels almost boring.

There is no dramatic confrontation. No triumphant speech. No cinematic exit. It is just steady refusal to play the old game.

Over time, one of three things happens.

1. They adjust and find a new rhythm with you.

2. They escalate for a while; realize they are not getting the reaction

3. They used to and eventually lose interest in pulling.

Or they never stop, which tells you something important about what the relationship was built on in the first place.

That information might hurt. It is also clarifying.

The Loneliness of Not Picking It Up

Dropping the rope when someone keeps pulling is lonely.

It is lonely to choose peace over familiarity. Lonely to stop performing for someone who preferred you activated. Lonely to realize that intensity was mistaken for intimacy.

There will be quiet where tension used to live. There will be space where you once filled every silence with explanation. There will be moments where you miss the chaos because at least chaos felt like connection.

That does not mean you made the wrong choice. It means you are grieving the version of the relationship that required you to shrink.

You are allowed to love someone and still refuse to yank the rope just to prove it.

You are allowed to stop playing tug-of-war even if the other person is still standing there, red-faced and determined.

One day you will walk away from an interaction that used to unravel you and realize you are not replaying it in the shower. You are not drafting imaginary rebuttals in your car. You are not mentally reopening the case at midnight.

You are just… done.

Not angry. Not superior. Not detached in a dramatic way. No longer available for the game.

That quiet shift, as unglamorous as it feels, is power. Not the loud kind. The kind that lets the rope fall to the ground between you and stay there.

10

THE MOMENT YOU FEEL THE PULL

What Happens in Your Body Before You Speak

There is a moment that matters more than the conversation itself, more than the words, more than the perfect response you rehearse later in the shower while winning an argument that already ended three hours ago.

It happens before you speak. Before you think clearly. Before you decide who is right.

It happens in your body.

Someone says something - maybe it's neutral, maybe it has a little edge - and your chest tightens like it just signed up for a CrossFit class without consulting you. Your jaw sets. Your shoulders inch forward like you're about to step into battle over something that, five minutes ago, did not matter to you at all.

Your nervous system doesn't wait for context. It does not request clarification. It does not raise its hand politely and ask for additional data.

It grabs a megaphone and screams, "We are under attack."

And now you're activated.

The fascinating part is that nothing objectively dramatic has happened yet. No one has insulted your ancestors. No one has revoked your citizenship. Someone simply asked a question or made a comment, and your body has decided this is a referendum on your competence, your integrity, and possibly your entire personality.

That's the pull.

The reason it feels so convincing is because it doesn't start in your thoughts. It starts in sensation. Tight chest. Heat rising. Slight forward lean. The urge to correct, clarify, and present a fully documented PowerPoint defense complete with charts and emotional footnotes.

You are not calmly evaluating the situation. You are three sentences into an explanation while still pretending you're "just responding."

Let's be honest. The pull does not only show up in serious moments. It shows up when someone texts "K." It shows up when your partner says, "That's not what you said earlier," and suddenly you feel like your credibility as a functioning adult is on the line. It shows up in the group chat when you share something vulnerable and the silence lasts slightly longer than your nervous system finds acceptable, and now you are mentally packing your belongings and moving to a small town where no one has Wi-Fi.

Your nervous system is dramatic. Not evil. Not broken. Dramatic.

It scans for threat constantly, and to it, threat does not mean physical harm. It means social harm. It means being misunderstood, misjudged, dismissed, or reduced to something you don't recognize as yourself.

So, when someone's tone lands sideways, your body hears, "They think you're lazy."

Or "They think you didn't try."

Or "They think you don't care."

Whether they actually think that is irrelevant. Your nervous system has already opened a case file and begun gathering evidence.

That's why urgency is the loudest symptom of the pull. Not the thought that you should respond, but the feeling that you must respond immediately or something irreversible will happen. Your brain starts generating reasons at lightning speed. If you don't clarify now, they'll believe the wrong thing. If you let it go, it will fester. If you don't defend yourself, this will become your reputation.

It feels responsible. Mature. Proactive.

It is adrenaline wearing a blazer.

When you act from that urgency, you're not being strategic. You're discharging stress. Your body wants relief, and explanation feels like relief. Defense feels like relief. Talking faster feels like relief.

But here's what is both humbling and liberating: almost nothing that feels urgent in a conversation actually is. The moment rarely explodes. The other person rarely solidifies a lifelong opinion about you in the span of twelve seconds. Most interactions pass if you let them breathe.

Which brings us to the pause.

The pause is not glamorous. It does not feel empowered. It feels like standing still when every instinct is screaming, "Move."

You feel the heat. You feel the tightening. You feel the words lining up behind your teeth like they've been waiting for this moment all day.

And you don't say them.

At first, that pause feels unnatural, almost irresponsible, like you are neglecting your duty as Defender of Your Own Character. You sit there thinking, "If I don't correct this, I am complicit in the misunderstanding."

But nothing catastrophic happens. The other person continues speaking, or they stop, or they pivot, or they clarify themselves without you needing to intervene. The room does not collapse. Your identity remains intact. The world does not file a complaint.

Your body slowly recalibrates. The heat cools. Your breathing deepens. The urgency loosens its grip.

In that recalibration, something radical happens. You realize the pull was a sensation, not a command.

You are allowed to feel activated without acting activated. You are allowed to experience defensiveness without launching a defense. You are allowed to sit in discomfort without scrambling to fix it.

This is not suppression. It's discernment.

Over time, you start catching the pull earlier. At first, you notice it after you've already responded and you're replaying the interaction thinking, "Why did I say all of that?" Then you catch it mid-sentence. Then you catch it before the words form.

Eventually, you feel the pull and think, "Oh. There you are," like recognizing an old friend who tends to overreact at family gatherings.

That recognition changes everything because the moment you feel the pull is not the problem. It's the opportunity. It's the split second where you decide whether this moment deserves your energy or whether your nervous system is staging a Broadway production over a line that barely warranted a raised eyebrow.

The humor here is important because it softens the shame. You are not weak for feeling the pull. You are human. Your body is wired to protect your identity as fiercely as it protects your physical safety.

But you are not obligated to obey every alarm.

Sometimes the bravest thing you can do is sit there, feel your heart racing, notice your jaw clenching, and choose not to perform the defense your body prepared for you.

Not because you don't care. It's because you care enough about your peace to let the moment pass without turning it into a trial.

And that - that small, quiet pause - is where your freedom begins.

11

WHEN YOU DO NEED
TO SAY SOMETHING

Clear, Calm, and Done

There is a very specific kind of silence that feels wise. It feels spacious. It feels like you just dodged a pointless argument and preserved your sanity. You walk away thinking, *That was growth.*

And then there is the other kind of silence.

The kind that sits in your throat like a stone. The kind that follows you into the shower. The kind that makes you replay the conversation at 11:47 p.m. while staring at the ceiling, constructing the speech you should have given in the moment but didn't because you were trying to be evolved.

If you've ever found yourself whisper-arguing in the car alone after a conversation where you said nothing, you already know the difference.

Dropping the rope does not mean muting yourself. It does not mean becoming the emotionally minimalist monk of your family, workplace, or friend group. It does not mean absorbing things that actually matter and calling it maturity.

It means learning to tell the difference between urgency and clarity.

Urgency feels buzzy. It feels like heat rising. It feels like, *Say something now or you'll explode.* Clarity feels different. It feels steady. It feels like something settled in your chest saying, *This needs to be named.*

When you need to say something from clarity, you are not trying to win. You are not trying to dominate the room. You are not trying to fix how the other person perceives you. You are not trying to prove you are reasonable, intelligent, thoughtful, self-aware, spiritually advanced, or misunderstood in a beautiful way.

You are naming something true because it matters. That is a very different energy.

Most of us were raised to believe that speaking up requires a preface. A disclaimer. A softening paragraph. A gentle reminder that we are not monsters before we dare to express a boundary. So, when we finally say something, we do not say the thing. We circle it like a nervous intern presenting to the board.

"I don't want this to come across the wrong way…"

"I totally understand your perspective…"

"I might be overreacting…"

"I'm not trying to be difficult…"

By the time we arrive at the actual point, everyone is tired, including us.

If we're honest, the cushioning is rarely for them. It's for us. It's an attempt to guarantee that no one walks away thinking poorly of us. Its rope disguised as politeness.

Here is the shift.

When you speak without the rope, you do not overbuild the sentence. You do not add scaffolding. You do not perform your humility. You say the thing.

"I'm not okay with that."

"That doesn't work for me."

"I don't want to continue this conversation."

"I see it differently."

And then you stop.

The first time you do this, your internal alarm system will behave as if you just insulted someone's grandmother. Your brain will scream, *That was abrupt. That was harsh. That was socially dangerous.* You will want to send a follow-up text clarifying that you are, in fact, still a kind person with a beating heart.

You might even draft it.

This is the part where humor saves you, because once you notice how dramatic your nervous system gets over one clear sentence, it becomes slightly absurd. You say, "That doesn't work for me," and your body responds like you just flipped a conference table in slow motion.

Nothing exploded.

No one fainted.

The sky remained in place.

Clarity often feels more extreme than it is because you are used to diluting yourself.

There is also this strange fear that if you do not explain yourself thoroughly, you will be misunderstood. That if you do not provide context, backstory, and emotional footnotes, someone will walk away with the wrong impression.

They might. That is not something you can control.

This is the part people do not want to hear: being understood is not guaranteed, even when you explain beautifully. You can deliver the most articulate, compassionate, self-aware explanation and someone can still decide you are wrong, cold, unreasonable, or dramatic.

The rope convinces you that more explanation equals more safety.

It does not. Sometimes it only equals more exhaustion.

When you speak from steadiness instead of activation, your body feels different. Your shoulders are not up around your ears. Your jaw is not tight. You are not leaning forward like you are about to enter battle. Your voice is slower. Your breathing is normal. You are not scanning their face for signs of approval.

You are not defending. You are stating.

There is power in that simplicity.

Sometimes saying something looks like naming the moment instead of reacting to it.

"This feels tense."

"I think we're starting to talk past each other."

"That landed differently than I think you intended."

Those sentences lower the temperature instead of raising it. They do not accuse. They observe.

Other times saying something looks like opting out without ceremony.

"I'm not going to keep going in circles."

"I've already answered that."

"I'm done discussing this."

And yes, that can feel wildly uncomfortable if you have built your identity around being the reasonable one, the communicator, the fixer, the smoother of awkward edges.

You will feel the urge to soften it. To add, "I just don't want this to turn into something…" or "I don't want you to think I'm upset…" or "I just think we should…"

You do not have to.

You are allowed to end a loop without delivering a TED Talk about why loops are inefficient.

Now here is the part that requires discipline.

When you speak clearly without the rope, some people will try to pull you back in. They may challenge your wording. They may ask follow-up questions that are not curious but strategic. They may say, "So you're saying I'm the problem?" even when you absolutely did not say that.

This is where most people collapse.

They rush to clarify. They scramble to reassure. They re-enter the debate because they cannot tolerate being misunderstood.

Sometimes the most grounded move is repetition.

"I'm not comfortable with that."

"I've already answered."

"I'm not changing my decision."

Not louder. Not sharper. Not longer.

Just the same.

Repetition without escalation is anchoring. It says, "I am not here to fight. I am not here to convince you. I am here to be clear."

You will feel awkward at first. It will feel like you are breaking an invisible social contract. But often that contract was built around you over-functioning and over-explaining.

This chapter is not about becoming blunt for sport. It is not about enjoying confrontation. It is about recognizing when silence would be self-abandonment and when speech would be self-defense dressed up as righteousness.

If you are speaking to protect your image, you are holding the rope.

If you are speaking to control the outcome, you are holding the rope.

If you are speaking because something true needs to be named and you can tolerate whatever reaction follows, you are not.

That tolerance is the key.

You do not get to control how your honesty lands. You only get to control whether you betray yourself trying to manage it.

Sometimes the most powerful sentence in a conversation is the one that is simple, clean, and followed by quiet. Not dramatic quiet. Not icy quiet. Just... quiet.

If you feel the urge to immediately fill that quiet because it is uncomfortable, ask yourself gently, *Am I clarifying... or am I pulling?*

When you can answer that honestly, you will know exactly what to do next.

12

ROPE- FREE RESPONSES

What to Say Without Getting Pulled Back In

There comes a moment when awareness alone is useless.

You see the rope. You feel the pull. You know exactly what's happening in your nervous system. And still - someone is standing in front of you waiting for an answer while your heart is racing like you just got drafted into emotional combat.

This is where insight isn't enough. This is where you need language.

Not clever comebacks.

Not therapy jargon.

Not a speech that sounds like you're applying for sainthood.

You need words that close the loop instead of tightening it. And here's the first thing to tattoo on the inside of your brain:

The longer the response, the tighter the rope.

Most of us don't get pulled back in because we're wrong. We get pulled back in because we keep talking. We explain until we accidentally argue. We clarify until we invalidate ourselves. We add context that invites debate. We soften so much that our boundary disappears.

Rope-free responses are boring on purpose.

They are not impressive.

They are not poetic.

They are not designed to win.

They are designed to end the pull.

And yes, at first, that feels anticlimactic. You've spent years thinking the "right" words would finally solve everything. They won't. The right *length* will.

When Someone Questions Your Choice

This is the classic rope. The one that hooks you because it sounds reasonable.

"Why would you do it that way?"

"Are you sure that's a good idea?"

"I just don't understand your thinking."

Your body hears: *Defend your competence.*

Your ego hears: *They think you're wrong.*

Your mouth wants to deliver a TED Talk.

Don't.

Try this instead:

"It works for me."

"I'm comfortable with my decision."

"I've thought it through."

And then stop.

Do not add the behind-the-scenes PowerPoint presentation. Do not walk them through your research process. Do not cite your emotional sources.

If they push again, repeat the sentence. Same tone. Same words.

Repetition is not aggression. It's closure.

When Someone Is Disappointed in You

This one hits straight in the chest.

"I guess I expected more."

"I thought I mattered."

"I'm just hurt."

Your nervous system screams: *Fix it. Repair it. Make them okay.*

But rope-free doesn't mean cold. It means clean.

"I hear that you're disappointed."

"I understand you wanted something different."

"I still made the choice I needed to make."

Notice what's not in there: apology tours, self-erasure, promises to overextend next time.

You can acknowledge feelings without negotiating your boundary.

That sentence alone will feel revolutionary.

When Someone Misreads Your Intent

"So, you just don't care?"

"Wow. That was cold."

"I guess this is who you are now."

This is where people spiral. Because we want to correct the story.

Here's the rule: Clarify once. Only once.

"That's not my intention."

"That's not how I see it."

"We're interpreting this differently."

Then let it sit.

If you explain beyond that, you're not clarifying - you're convincing.

Convincing is tug-of-war in a blazer.

When They Use "I'm Just Being Honest"

This is the emotional version of "no offense."

"I'm just being honest."

"Someone has to say it."

You do not owe your nervous system to someone else's unfiltered opinion.

"You can be honest without being disrespectful."

"I'm open to feedback, not to that tone."

"If you want a real conversation, we can do that."

Short. Steady. Done.

When They Keep Interrupting

Nothing activates faster than being talked over. It's like your nervous system has been waiting its whole life to say, *See? No one listens to you.*

Instead of escalating:

"Let me finish."

"I'm not done speaking."

"If we're going to talk, we take turns."

You do not need to raise your voice. Calm repetition is unnerving in the best way.

When They Won't Take "No"

Some people treat "no" like an opening offer.

"Are you sure?"

"Come on."

"Just this once."

Here's the rope: the urge to justify.

Instead:

"I've answered."

"My answer isn't changing."

"You don't have to like it. I would like you to respect it."

You will feel powerful and slightly illegal saying that last one. It's fine.

You're allowed.

When You Feel Yourself Slipping

This one matters most.

You start strong, clear, and centered. Then, you hear your voice speed up. You feel yourself adding context. You sense the rope tightening in real time.

That's when you stop mid-conversation. Literally.

Then, you say this:

"I'm going to pause here."

"Let me stop myself."

"I don't want to keep explaining."

That's not awkward. That's self-awareness in motion.

It may feel exposed the first few times, like you just admitted you're human. You are. Congratulations.

The Texting Rope

Texting deserves its own chapter, but here we are.

Someone replies with "K." And suddenly you're analyzing one letter like it's encrypted.

You draft three responses. Delete. Rewrite. Add an exclamation point you don't feel so you seem relaxed.

This is the rope with Wi-Fi.

Rope-free texting looks like: Answering the actual question. Not following up to manage tone.

Letting silence sit. Do not respond immediately just because you can.

If you draft a long message and feel your chest tight - save it. Come back in an hour. Most of the time you won't send it. You'll be grateful you didn't.

The text you don't send is often the rope you didn't pick up.

The Social Media Rope

This is where rope gets an audience.

You post something. Someone comments sideways. Not aggressive. Just… pointed.

Your body lights up. You feel the urge to clarify for the imaginary crowd watching.

Here's the truth: most of the crowd is not watching.

Rope-free on social media looks like:

Not responding to bait.

Deleting without announcing.

Turning off comments.

Unfollowing without guilt.

Logging off.

You do not owe strangers your nervous system.

When You Need to End It

Sometimes you need to close it cleanly.

"I'm done with this conversation."

"This isn't productive for me."

"I'm stepping away."

No drama. No door slam. Just finality.

Then follow through.

The power of rope-free language isn't in the sentence. It's in the consistency.

The Hardest Hack

You do not have to convince anyone.

If your response is designed to finally make them agree, soften, understand, approve, validate, or stop being uncomfortable - you are still pulling.

Rope-free responses are about alignment, not agreement.

You are not here to win the room. You are here to stay intact.

Expect This (So You Don't Panic)

When you start responding this way:

Some people will calm down.

Some will escalate.

Some will act confused.

Some will accuse you of changing.

That doesn't mean your words were wrong. It means the old dynamic is losing oxygen.

Stay steady.

Stay brief.

Stay boring.

Boring is underrated. Boring is rope-proof.

You don't need perfect lines. You need grounded ones.

Use these. Adapt them. Make them sound like you. But don't turn them into speeches. The rope tightens with every extra sentence.

Now you know exactly when to stop talking.

13

AFTER THE CONVERSATION

When Your Brain Wants to Reopen the Case

The conversation ends.

You walk away. You hang up. You set your phone face down on the counter like someone who just survived a hostage negotiation and would like a medal. You didn't overexplain. You didn't spiral. You didn't grab the rope. You stayed steady. You said what needed to be said. You stopped when it was time to stop.

For approximately eleven seconds, you feel like a fully evolved adult.

And then your brain clocks back in like an unpaid intern who refuses to leave the office.

It starts small. Subtle. Reasonable.

Was that too blunt?

Maybe I should've added one more sentence.

What if they took that the wrong way?

What if I sounded cold?

What if I am cold?

Suddenly, you're not in your kitchen anymore. You're back in the conversation; except this time, you're editing it like a director's cut of your own life. You replay the tone. The pause. The micro-expression you swear you saw flash across their face. You reconstruct the scene with smoother phrasing, softer delivery, a version where you are firm but warm and wise and somehow also charismatic enough that they walk away thinking, "Wow, that was the healthiest boundary I've ever seen."

That's the rope. Only quieter.

This is where most people undo their progress. Not in the moment. After it.

In the moment, you were clear. After it, you become your own opposition counsel. You cross-examine yourself. You question your tone. You interrogate your intent. You wonder if you accidentally committed emotional manslaughter by not cushioning your truth in enough disclaimers.

You don't reopen the case because the other person asked for clarification. You reopen it because discomfort showed up.

You have spent a lifetime relieving discomfort by explaining.

The Follow-Up Text Temptation

You know this move.

You did fine in the conversation. You said your piece. It ended. And then, forty minutes later, you're holding your phone, typing:

"Just to clarify what I meant earlier…"

"Sorry if that came across wrong…"

"I just want to make sure you know I didn't mean…"

Nobody asked.

There was no new development. No new harm. No follow-up question. Just you and your nervous system having a hard time with unresolved tension.

The follow-up text feels productive. Mature. Responsible.

It is often none of those things. It is self-soothing in disguise.

Listen - that's not a moral failure. That's a nervous system trying to return to baseline. Your brain hates open loops. It hates unfinished stories. It wants certainty. It wants approval. It wants everyone to understand you exactly the way you intended.

Real life does not provide that kind of editing control.

Most conversations end slightly unfinished. Slightly imperfect. Slightly ambiguous.

You survive them anyway.

The Courtroom in Your Head

After the conversation, your brain becomes a courtroom drama with zero commercial breaks.

Exhibit A: The sentence you used.

Exhibit B: The facial expression they made.

Exhibit C: The tone you *think* you heard in their response.

You build a case against yourself.

Maybe I should have softened that.

Maybe I should have been more empathetic.

Maybe I sounded defensive.

Maybe I made it worse.

You are simultaneously the defendant, the prosecutor, and the judge. The jury is made up of imaginary people whose opinions you are trying to control.

It is exhausting.

Here's the kicker - none of them are actually present. The conversation is over and the only person still arguing is you.

That's the rope turning inward.

The Addiction to Being Understood

Part of you wants to be right. But a deeper part wants to be understood.

When you walk away from a conversation without a neat bow on it, your system panics. Because being misunderstood feels like being misjudged. Being misjudged feels like being rejected. And rejection, to your nervous system, feels like danger.

So, it pushes you to fix it.

Clarify it.

Reframe it.

Add context.

Explain your heart better.

You think you're protecting the relationship. You are often protecting your image inside their mind.

You cannot control the version of you that lives in someone else's head. You can only control whether you abandon yourself trying.

The Itch of Unfinished

The first few times you don't send the follow-up, it feels itchy.

Physically itchy.

You'll open your phone. You'll type something. You'll delete it. You'll open it again. You'll stare at the thread like it's going to start speaking back to you.

Nothing happens.

No explosion.

No emergency.

No public shaming campaign.

The world continues spinning, completely indifferent to your internal spiral. That is the moment your nervous system learns something new.

Silence did not equal danger.

Unfinished did not equal disaster.

Discomfort did not require action.

That is not small. That is rewiring.

Is There New Information... or Only Discomfort?

This question is your lifeline:

Is there new information - or only discomfort?

If something new happened, address it.

If harm was caused, repair it.

If you genuinely mis-stepped, own it.

If nothing new occurred and your only driver is the feeling that you might be misunderstood, you are not responding to reality. You are responding to anxiety.

Anxiety is loud. It is persuasive. It sounds like responsibility.

It is not the same thing.

You do not need to preemptively clean up a mess that does not exist.

The Guilt Voice

After a rope-free response, guilt often shows up dressed as virtue.

You should have been softer.

You could have been more patient.

Maybe you were selfish.

Maybe you made it about you.

That voice feels familiar because it kept you safe once. Over-accommodating probably helped you survive something. It helped you maintain peace. It helped you belong.

It does not get to run the show anymore.

Growth will always feel slightly rude to the version of you that survived by over-explaining.

That doesn't mean it's wrong.

The Fantasy Edit

There is also the fantasy edit.

You replay the conversation and imagine the improved version. The one where you're calm and eloquent and slightly witty and everyone leaves thinking you're emotionally advanced and spiritually hydrated.

You don't need that version. You need the real one.

The one where you were steady enough.

Clear enough.

Done enough.

You are not performing communication for applause. You are participating in it as a human.

Humans do not get perfect edits.'

When It Actually Needs Revisiting

Let's be clear. Some conversations deserve repair.

If you snapped. If you lashed out. If you grabbed the rope and used it as a weapon. If you said something misaligned with your values - go back. Repair is strength.

Revisiting is not the same as polishing.

Repair addresses harm.

Polishing addresses ego.

Know the difference.

Letting It Be Enough

Dropping the rope after the conversation is about trust.

Trusting that clarity does not require micromanagement.

Trusting that being misunderstood sometimes is survivable.

Trusting that silence is neutral, not dangerous.

Trusting that if something truly needs clarification, the other person will ask.

You do not need to hover over every interaction like it's a soufflé that might collapse if you stop watching it.

Most conversations are not soufflés. They are microwaved leftovers. Imperfect and fine.

Let what you said be enough.

Let the unfinished stay unfinished.

Let your nervous system learn that you do not have to chase every flicker of discomfort with a paragraph.

The rope after the conversation is subtle.

It doesn't look like tug-of-war.

It looks like rumination.

Rumination is just tug-of-war with yourself.

You don't have to win the replay.

You only have to stop pressing play.

Next we'll talk about the inevitable moment when you do grab the rope again, when you overexplain, when you react faster than you meant to - because you will - and why that does not cancel everything you just learned.

You are not trying to become rope-proof. You are learning how to let go - even after the room is quiet.

PART IV

LIVING IT

14

WHEN YOU SLIP
AND GRAB THE ROPE

Progress Is Faster Recovery, Not Perfection

You will mess this up.

Not once in a dramatic, cinematic way where you vow to do better and then magically do. Not occasionally in a way that makes you feel mildly annoyed with yourself. Repeatedly. In normal conversations. On random Tuesdays. In texts that start out harmless and end with you three paragraphs deep explaining why you prefer oat milk.

You will notice the rope. You will swear you are not touching it. You will internally congratulate yourself for being evolved and regulated and above this nonsense. And then you will hear your own voice, mid-sentence, explaining something you already decided did not need explaining.

You will think, *Oh no. I am doing it again.*

Yes. You are.

This chapter exists so that moment does not turn into a verdict about who you are as a human being.

Slipping is not a moral failure. It is not proof that you are doomed to over-explain forever. It is not evidence that you "haven't healed enough." It is what happens when a nervous system that practiced one pattern for decades tries to install a new one in real time while someone is staring at it.

You are rewiring, not replacing a lightbulb.

The Fantasy That Sets You Up

There is a quiet fantasy people bring into this work, and it sounds inspiring until it betrays you.

The fantasy is that once you see the pattern, you will never fall into it again. That awareness flips a permanent switch. That you will now float through life serene and rope-free like some emotionally enlightened monk who does not care what anyone thinks.

This fantasy feels motivating. It is actually brutal.

The first time you slip, that fantasy turns into a weapon.

See? I knew it.

I am still reactive.

Why can't I just stay calm?

I thought I was past this.

Now you are not only pulling rope in the conversation. You are pulling rope with yourself afterward.

That inner commentary is just another tug-of-war. It sounds like accountability, but it is shame wearing business casual.

Change is not linear. It is not a staircase. It is more like trying to teach your dog a new trick while your dog occasionally forgets English and reverts to barking at the wind.

You do not wake up fluent in a language you have been speaking wrong your whole life. You catch yourself mid-sentence. You stumble. You backtrack. You wince. You learn.

The fact that you notice the stumble faster now is progress, even if it feels like embarrassment.

What Actually Happened When You Slipped

Let's slow this down, because your brain may try to dramatize it.

You were doing well. Maybe for days. Maybe for weeks. You were noticing the rope. You were choosing differently. You were feeling steadier. You were quietly impressed with yourself.

Then something shifted.

You were tired.

Hungry.

Stressed.

Ambushed.

Talking to someone who knows your childhood nickname and exactly which buttons to press.

Your capacity dropped.

When capacity drops, your nervous system does not politely ask for your long-term growth goals. It defaults to what it knows.

That is not weakness. That is biology.

Your nervous system has default settings. When resources are low, it reverts to the pattern that once kept you safe. Explaining kept you safe. Defending kept you safe. Over-clarifying kept you safe.

So, when your brain senses threat and your capacity is thin, it says, "Ah yes. We know this one. Begin explanation mode."

That is neuroscience, not character flaw.

The slip did not happen because you are broken. It happened because you are human and under-resourced in that moment.

Compassion here is not indulgence. It is strategy. The faster you move through shame, the faster you return to practice.

The Self-Punishment Spiral

Here is where people make it worse.

They slip. They grab the rope. They over-explain. They get defensive. They say too much. The conversation ends.

Then they spend the next six hours replaying it like a director who hates their own movie.

Why did I say that?

Why did I keep talking?

I should have stopped sooner.

I am never going to get this right.

This feels productive. It feels like accountability. It feels like if you criticize yourself hard enough, you will scare yourself into doing better next time.

It does not work that way.

Shame does not motivate change. Shame freezes you and makes you defensive, not with others, but with yourself. When you are defending yourself to yourself, you are not learning anything. You are just punishing.

The better move is painfully simple.

You grabbed the rope.

Okay. What now?

Not what is wrong with me.

Just what now.

That question moves you forward. The other one keeps you circling.

Slipping Versus Staying

There is a critical difference between slipping and staying.

Slipping is grabbing the rope.

Staying is refusing to let go once you have it in your hands.

Slipping happens fast. Staying is a choice.

You are mid-explanation. You feel the tightness in your chest. You hear your tone rising. You realize you are arguing for a point you already decided did not need defending.

You can keep going because you are already in it.

Or you can stop. Even if it is awkward. Even if it is mid-sentence.

"Let me pause here."

"Actually, I don't need to explain all of that."

"I'm going to stop myself."

That is not failure. That is recovery in real time.

You do not owe anyone a smooth exit. You owe yourself honesty.

The skill is not never grabbing the rope. The skill is putting it down faster.

The High-Risk Zones

You will notice certain situations hook you harder.

Family gatherings where everyone silently reverts to their childhood roles like it is a reunion tour nobody asked for.

Work meetings where someone questions your competence and your nervous system lights up like a Christmas tree.

Text threads where tone is ambiguous and your imagination does gymnastics.

These are not random. They are high-risk zones.

If you know family dinners tend to activate you, do not walk in expecting to be emotionally invincible. Walk in knowing the rope will show up and having a plan for when it does.

If you know you are more reactive when exhausted, do not schedule hard conversations at 9:30 p.m. after a day that felt like a marathon run in dress shoes.

This is not avoidance. This is capacity management.

You are not trying to be perfect. You are trying to be prepared.

The Over-Correction Trap

After a slip, there is often a dramatic urge to swing the other direction.

You over-explained, so now you become silent and cold. You reacted emotionally, so now you detach completely. You engaged a dynamic you did not want, so now you cut the person off entirely.

This feels decisive. It is usually just the pendulum swinging.

Over-correction is still reaction. You are still being controlled by the moment, just in reverse.

Dropping the rope after a slip does not mean swinging to the opposite extreme. It means returning to center.

No punishment. No dramatic exits. No vows to "never care again."

Just center.

The Urge to Fix It

Sometimes after you slip, you want to go back and redo the scene.

You want to send the follow-up message that clarifies what you "actually meant." You want to have the conversation again but better. You want to correct the tone and polish the edges, so it looks like you meant to be composed all along.

Ask yourself one hard question: Is this repair or relief?

If you caused harm, repair it. That is strength.

If you just feel uncomfortable with how imperfect you were, that is relief you are chasing.

Most of the time, the cleanest recovery is doing nothing.

Let the messy moment stay messy.

Let the other person think whatever they are thinking.

Let yourself be human in someone else's story.

What Recovery Actually Looks Like

Recovery is not dramatic. It is not a declaration. It is not a vow.

It is quiet.

It is noticing you grabbed the rope and choosing not to build a shame monument about it.

It is catching yourself mid-pull and stopping, even if it feels abrupt.

It is adjusting your expectations for high-risk situations instead of expecting yourself to be unshakeable.

It is treating the slip as information instead of identity.

It is not texting the person three hours later to explain what you "really meant."

It is getting back to practice in the next interaction.

That is recovery.

Not polished. Not perfect. Only intentional.

The Timeline Nobody Tells You

Progress in this work does not look like a straight line. It looks like layers.

At first, you notice the rope hours later.

Then you notice it at the end of the conversation.

Then you notice it mid-conversation but cannot quite stop.

Then you notice it and stop mid-sentence.

Then, occasionally, you notice it before you grab it.

Most people expect to jump straight to the final stage.

They do not.

You cycle through all of them. Sometimes in the same week.

Slipping does not mean you are back at zero. It means you are somewhere in the middle of learning.

That is not regression. That is repetition.

Repetition is how skills are built.

The Slip That Teaches You

Sometimes a slip is clarifying.

You thought you were past reacting to a certain person. You slip, grab the rope, and realize, oh, this dynamic still has hooks.

Good. Now you know. That is information.

It tells you where the edge still is. It shows you where more awareness is needed. It gives you data about your capacity, your triggers, your unfinished stories.

Information is not shame. It is leverage.

Progress Is Not Perfection

The goal was never to stop being human. The goal was to stop being controlled by automatic patterns you did not choose.

You are still going to care. You are still going to get activated. You are still going to have moments where your mouth moves faster than your intention.

That is not a glitch. That is life.

The only question that matters after a slip is this:

Do you stay in the pull, or do you recover?

Every time you choose recovery, even imperfectly, you are strengthening the skill that eventually becomes your baseline.

You do not need to be rope-proof.

You need to be willing to drop it again.

And again.

And again.

That is not failure. That is practice.

15

LIVING ROPE-FREE

Ordinary Peace Is the Point

Living rope-free does not look like incense smoke and enlightenment quotes. It does not look like you floating through conflict with wind in your hair and a perfectly regulated vagus nerve. It looks like you standing in your kitchen, someone commenting on the size of your frying pan, and you not launching into a defense brief like you're presenting to the Supreme Court of Breakfast.

That is far more radical than it sounds.

Most of your exhaustion was never about the actual conflict. It was about the performance. The rehearsing. The preparing. The pre-emptive defense of choices no one formally accused you of making wrong. You were living like there was always a panel of judges in the room grading your tone, your reasoning, your posture, your milk choice, your calendar, your parenting, your personality.

Living rope-free means you quietly retire the panel.

You don't announce it. You don't post about it. You just

stop showing up to the courtroom.

What Actually Changes

Six months in, a year in, something subtle starts happening that you don't even recognize at first.

You walk into a room, and you are not braced. You do not mentally inventory who might say something sideways. You do not draft responses in advance to questions that haven't been asked.

You are simply… there.

It feels suspicious at first, like you forgot something important. Like you left the oven on. Your body keeps waiting for the familiar spike of "prepare yourself." And when it doesn't come, you almost go looking for it out of habit. You've been living in low-grade anticipatory defense for so long that calm feels irresponsible.

But then you realize you are not tired after conversations the way you used to be.

You are not replaying someone's tone while brushing your teeth. You are not writing an imaginary email in your head while trying to fall asleep.

You had the conversation. It ended. And your brain did not reopen it like a true-crime podcast titled *The Case of What I Should Have Said.*

That is not small. That is freedom disguised as ordinary.

The Frying Pan, Revisited

Let's go back to the pan that I brought up in Chapter One.

Same kitchen. Same stovetop. Same comment that once would have activated a full internal symposium.

"Is that pan big enough?"

Old you would have felt the micro-spike. The implication. The subtle suggestion that maybe you did not plan properly, maybe you underestimated, maybe you are once again proving the theory that you are almost competent but not quite.

Old you would have responded with a thesis.

"Yes, it's fine, I only need it for a few eggs, and the larger one takes longer to heat and honestly it's more efficient this way and I've done this before and -"

You know the rest.

Living rope-free looks like this:

"Yep."

You flip the eggs.

You do not explain your pan strategy like it's an architectural decision.

You do not narrate your competence. You let the comment land and dissolve.

You dare yourself to see what happens when you do not defend.

What happens?

Nothing.

The eggs cook.

The earth keeps rotating.

No one files a report.

The room does not collapse under the weight of your insufficient cookware.

You discover that most of the tension you were managing was hypothetical.

The Way You Listen Now

Something else shifts, and this one sneaks up on you: You start actually hearing people.

Before, you were listening for danger. For subtext. For the moment your character might be questioned. Conversations were chess matches and you were constantly calculating your next move, tracking perception like it was oxygen.

Now, because your worth is not on trial, you can let people finish sentences.

You can sit in pauses without assuming the pause is judgment.

You can hear criticism without immediately translating it into indictment.

Sometimes you still feel the flicker of activation, but it does not own you. It rises. You notice it. You do not immediately mobilize. It's like watching a storm cloud form and choosing not to run inside screaming that the weather is personal.

You become easier to talk to, not because you are agreeable, but because you are not armored.

That unsettles some people. That becomes toleration without the expense of you.

How Relationships Reorganize

This is where it gets interesting.

When you stop pulling, relationships reveal their actual structure.

Some deepen because they were never built on tension to begin with. They were built on mutual respect that got buried under your constant explaining. When you stop performing, those relationships breathe like they've been waiting for you to unclench.

Some loosen because they were quietly organized around your over-functioning. Around your availability. Around your emotional labor. When you stop providing the fuel, the engine sputters. It does not mean the relationship was fake. It means it required you to strain in order to operate.

Some disappear entirely.

Here is the part that feels edgy and slightly rebellious: you let them.

Not with drama. Not with a speech about growth. Just with a shrug and a recognition that if the only way the relationship worked was through friction and intensity and emotional tug-of-war, then removing the rope removes the glue.

You are not collecting relationships anymore. You are choosing alignment.

I dare you to try that.

The Space That Opens

You do not realize how much mental bandwidth you were burning until you get it back.

The hours you used to spend replaying tone now become actual hours.

The energy you used to invest in drafting imaginary defenses becomes energy you can use to create, to rest, to show up fully somewhere else.

You start noticing things you missed before because you were too busy defending yourself in your own head. The way sunlight hits the kitchen counter. The way your kid tells a story without you half-listening while constructing rebuttals to something someone said earlier.

You become present.

Not in a mystical way but in a practical way.

You are not multitasking your own defense while living your life.

When the Pull Still Shows Up

Let's not romanticize this. You will still feel it sometimes.

Someone will make a comment that lands crooked. Someone will misread you. Someone will imply something that pokes an old nerve.

The pull will flicker.

The difference is that now it feels optional.

You notice the tightening. You notice the urge to correct. And instead of obeying it like a command, you pause and think, "Is this worth my energy?"

Sometimes the answer is yes, and you speak clearly from steadiness. Sometimes the answer is no, and you let it go.

The power is not in always choosing silence. The power is in knowing you are choosing.

What People Notice

Some people will tell you that you seem calmer.

Others will tell you that you have changed.

Some will say you are more grounded.

Some will say you are harder to reach.

All of them are correct.

You are calmer because you are not constantly braced.

You have changed because you stopped performing.

You are harder to reach if reaching you used to mean hooking you into reactivity.

That is not cruelty. That is clarity.

The Internal Doubt

There will be moments when you wonder if you are being too firm. Too distant. Too unbothered.

You will occasionally miss the intensity. The adrenaline. The weird sense of connection that comes from heated back-and-forth. Because your nervous system once equated activation with aliveness.

Living rope-free can feel boring at first. Boring is terrifying to people who are used to chaos feeling like intimacy.

I dare you to sit in that boredom.

On the other side of it is stability.

The Real Flex

The real flex is not the perfect boundary statement.

It is not the clever response nor the mic-drop line.

The real flex is cooking eggs in the pan you chose without narrating your reasoning.

It is answering a question without building a case.

It is letting someone misunderstand you without launching a campaign to correct it.

It is walking away from a conversation and not reopening it in your head for a post-game analysis.

It is not needing to win.

That kind of strength does not look impressive on Instagram.

It looks like Tuesday. And Tuesday is where you live.

The Dare

You picked up this book because you were possibly tired.

Tired of defending your choices.

Tired of explaining your tone.

Tired of caring about things that should not have taken up that much space.

You thought the rope was protection.

It wasn't. It was habit.

You do not have to grab it every time it is offered.

You can see it. Feel the pull. Notice the urge rising like a reflex you have known your whole life. You can dare yourself to leave it on the floor.

Not perfectly.

Not every time.

Just enough.

Enough to see what happens when you stop arguing for your right to exist.

Enough to feel what it is like to stand in a room without bracing.

Enough to realize that most of the battles you were fighting were imaginary juries you appointed yourself.

So, here is the final invitation, and I mean it:

The next time someone questions the pan, the plan, the tone, the timeline, the milk choice, the calendar, the life choice you made that makes perfect sense to you but apparently requires explanation in the wild -

pause.

Smile if you want. Answer if you need to. Then dare yourself not to explain.

See what happens when you do not pick up the rope.

You might discover something slightly dangerous.

You were never as fragile as you thought.

You were never required to perform in order to be enough.

Drop it.

Not dramatically.

Just… drop it.

Then go live your Tuesday.

PART V

THE PLAYBOOK

16

THE ROPE-FREE PLAYBOOK

Quick Tools for Real Moments

There comes a moment in this work where insight isn't enough.

You don't need another explanation about your nervous system. You don't need a reminder that you were misunderstood at age nine. You need something you can use when your jaw tightens, and your brain starts drafting a speech that was never requested.

This is that section.

This is the part you flip to when you're about to "just clarify one thing" and suddenly it's been eight minutes and you're explaining your entire personality to someone who asked a casual question.

This is execution.

The 10-Second Reset

Before you respond, text, clarify, defend, or add "just one more thing," do this:

135

Unclench your jaw.

Drop your shoulders.

Lean back instead of forward.

Take one slow inhale and one slow exhale.

If your body is leaning forward, you are about to grab the rope. If your voice is speeding up, you are already holding it.

Steady body. Then steady words.

You do not need to respond at the speed of your adrenaline.

When a Comment Lands Sideways

You know the kind. It's not an attack. It's a tone. A pause. An "interesting." A sentence that technically could mean anything but somehow lands directly on your nervous system.

Instead of launching into a defense or internally building a courtroom-level argument, try:

"Was that meant to help me or hurt me?"

"Can you say more about what you meant?"

"I'm not sure how to take that - what were you hoping I'd hear?"

Say it calmly. Not with an eyebrow raised. And not with a smirk.

People who meant well will clarify. People who meant harm will squirm.

Either way, you get clarity before you start fighting a war over something that may not require one.

When Someone Is Venting and You Feel the Fix-It Reflex Rising

They start talking and suddenly your brain opens fifteen tabs titled Solutions. You're assembling advice, restructuring their life, drafting a three-step plan like you're about to earn a certification in Emotional Logistics.

Pause.

Try:

"Do you want help solving this, or do you need to vent?"

"Are we problem-solving or processing?"

"What would feel most helpful from me right now?"

That question alone prevents you from over-functioning yourself into resentment.

You are not a 24-hour emotional repair shop. You are allowed to clarify your role before volunteering for labor that was never assigned to you.

When Someone Pushes Your Boundary

Instead of explaining your boundary until you're tired, thirsty, and wondering why you're defending your right to exist:

"What part of what I said feels unclear?"

"I've already answered that - is there something new here?"

"Help me understand what you're asking for now."

No speech.

No emotional essay.

No added context you hope will soften it.

If you repeat yourself calmly and they keep pushing, that's not a communication problem. That's data.

You don't need to escalate. You can disengage.

When You Feel Blamed

Instead of defending your entire character, your upbringing, and your intentions in one breath:

"What specifically are you saying I did?"

"Are we talking about behavior, or about who I am?"

"What outcome are you hoping for here?"

Vague blame survives because we panic and overexplain. Specific questions slow the room down.

You are not required to defend against accusations that aren't clearly defined.

When the Conversation Starts Looping

You feel it. The same words. The same tone. The same point being repackaged like it's new.

Name it.

"Are we repeating ourselves?"

"What would resolve this for you?"

"Is there something new we're trying to get to?"

Loops continue because nobody is brave enough to say, "We've already done this."

You can be that person. Calmly.

When It's Time to Stop Participating

Not every rope deserves technique.

If the tone shifts into mockery.

If you've repeated yourself twice.

If your body is escalating despite your effort.

If the conversation feels less like connection and more like a performance review you didn't schedule.

You can say:

"I'm not going to keep doing this."

"This isn't productive."

"We're not getting anywhere."

And then stop.

No exit monologue.

No closing argument.

No follow-up text later to "clarify."

Disengagement is not immaturity. It's discernment.

The Energy Test

Before you engage, ask:

Is this worth my energy?

Not:

Am I right?

Will they misunderstand me?

Should I correct this?

But:

Is this worth the cost of activation?

You can be completely correct and still decide it's not worth the adrenaline spike.

Peace sometimes looks like letting someone be wrong about you.

The Micro-Delay

When you feel pressure to respond immediately:

"Let me think about that."

"I'll get back to you."

"I'm not ready to answer that."

You are allowed to buy yourself time.

Urgency is often just the rope dressed up in a suit pretending to be responsibility.

What Not To Do

When you feel the pull, do not:

Send the "Just to clarify..." text that is actually three paragraphs long.

Add one more sentence to your email because you're afraid they'll misunderstand you.

Apologize for having a boundary.

Reopen a conversation that already ended because you're uncomfortable.

Try to land perfectly.

If there is no new information, it does not need new words.

Most follow-up messages are not about clarity. They're about self-soothing.

Be honest about which one you're doing.

The Rope Audit (Afterward)

Later, when you're alone and tempted to replay the moment in the shower:

Did I defend something that wasn't under attack?

Did I explain more than necessary?

Did I try to manage how I was perceived?

Did I stay connected to myself?

No shame spiral. No dramatic internal lecture. Just information.

Progress isn't about never grabbing the rope again. It's about noticing faster and dropping it sooner.

The Quiet Truth

You will not use these perfectly. You will still over-explain sometimes. You will still catch yourself mid-sentence and think, here we go again.

That's fine.

The goal was never to become untouchable. It was to become intentional.

When you can pause long enough to choose instead of react, you are living rope-free.

You don't need better comebacks.

You don't need to win.

You don't need to glow.

You need to stop grabbing the rope every time your nervous system twitches.

That's growth.

Not flashy.

Not dramatic.

Just solid.

And solid lasts.

You need to drop the rope.

When you do, you'll realize something surprising: you were never holding it to protect yourself. You were holding it because you forgot you could let go.

Now you know.

So, drop it and see what happens next.

Keep the Conversation Going

If parts of this book felt a little too familiar... you're not alone.

Every week I write a short newsletter called **ShiFt Happens**. It's where I share honest reflections about communication, relationships, emotions, and the everyday moments where life gets a little messy and our brains try to drag us back into the rope.

Sometimes it's about conversations.

Sometimes it's about people.

Sometimes it's just about being human.

No motivational fluff.

No recycled advice.

It's real-life insight and practical psychology you can actually use.

If that sounds like something you'd enjoy, you can join here:

readshifthappens.kit.com

Or scan the QR code below.

Takes about 10 seconds. No spam. Just the weekly ShiFt Happens email. I'd love for you to join us.

— Dr. Renea Skelton

ACKNOWLEDGMENTS

This book was not written in a quiet cabin with herbal tea and perfect boundaries.

It was written in real life. In kitchens. In hotels. In parked cars. After conversations I replayed too long. After moments I handled well - and plenty I didn't.

To my family - you have seen me at my best and at my most "why did I say that?" Thank you for loving me when I was gripping the rope like it was my job. You have given me room to grow without shaming me for how long it took... or how many times I needed to practice.

To my sister - thank you for being part of my story long before this book ever existed. Sisters have a way of knowing exactly which buttons to push... and which ropes we are still holding. I'm grateful for the history we share and the ways we continue to grow.

To the women I coached - you are the reason this exists. You show up exhausted from being the strong one. You whisper things out loud that you've carried for years. You have let me sit in the messy middle with you. This book carries your bravery. Not your names - but your courage.

To my military family - 22.5 years in the Air Force taught me how to stand tall, speak clearly, and lead under pressure. It also taught me how easy it is to confuse control with strength. Some of my biggest lessons about dropping the rope did not happen in conference rooms. They happened afterward... when the room was quiet and my ego was still arguing.

To my sister-in-arms and friend, Janelle, who wrote the foreword - thank you for reading this and seeing the weight of it. Your words matter. Your integrity matters. I am forever grateful.

And to you - the reader.

If you have ever walked away from a conversation and thought of seventeen better comebacks in the shower...

If you've ever defended yourself to someone who was not even listening...

If you've ever won the argument and still felt tired...

You are not dramatic. You are human.

And if this book helps you drop the rope even once when your brain is begging you to pick it back up... then every word was worth it.

Thank you for trusting me with this.

ABOUT THE AUTHOR

Dr. Renea Skelton did not set out to become someone who writes about dropping ropes.

She became someone who needed to.

At seventeen, she enlisted in the United States Air Force and spent the next 22.5 years learning how to lead, how to stay steady under pressure, and how to carry responsibility without flinching. She eventually commissioned as an officer, because apparently "go big or go home" was already part of her wiring.

Leadership came naturally. Letting go did not.

After retiring from the military, she shifted from commanding rooms to sitting in them differently. Today, she is a communication expert and nationally recognized keynote speaker who spends much of her time on stages and in workshops helping leaders, teams, and women communicate with clarity, handle conflict without losing themselves, and stop carrying battles that were never theirs to win.

She is also the award-winning author of *The Adventures of Henry the Hedgehog* children's book series, because emotional intelligence shouldn't wait until adulthood - and because sometimes it's easier to talk about big feelings when a hedgehog is involved.

Her work blends psychology, lived experience, and dry humor. She believes peace is not passive. It's practiced. Often imperfectly.

She lives in Texas. She still occasionally thinks of better comebacks hours later. And she still chooses, again and again, to drop the rope.

Learn more at www.reneaskelton.com